GETTING OFF ON 96

and other less traveled roads

DENNIS BLEYTHING
AND SUSAN HAWKINS

Drives and Hikes in the Trinity Alps, Redwoods and Siskiyous

The Touchstone Press
P.O. Box 81
Beaverton, Oregon 97005

Library of Congress
Catalog Card No. 75-9248
I.S.B.N. No. 0-911518-32-0

contents

area map

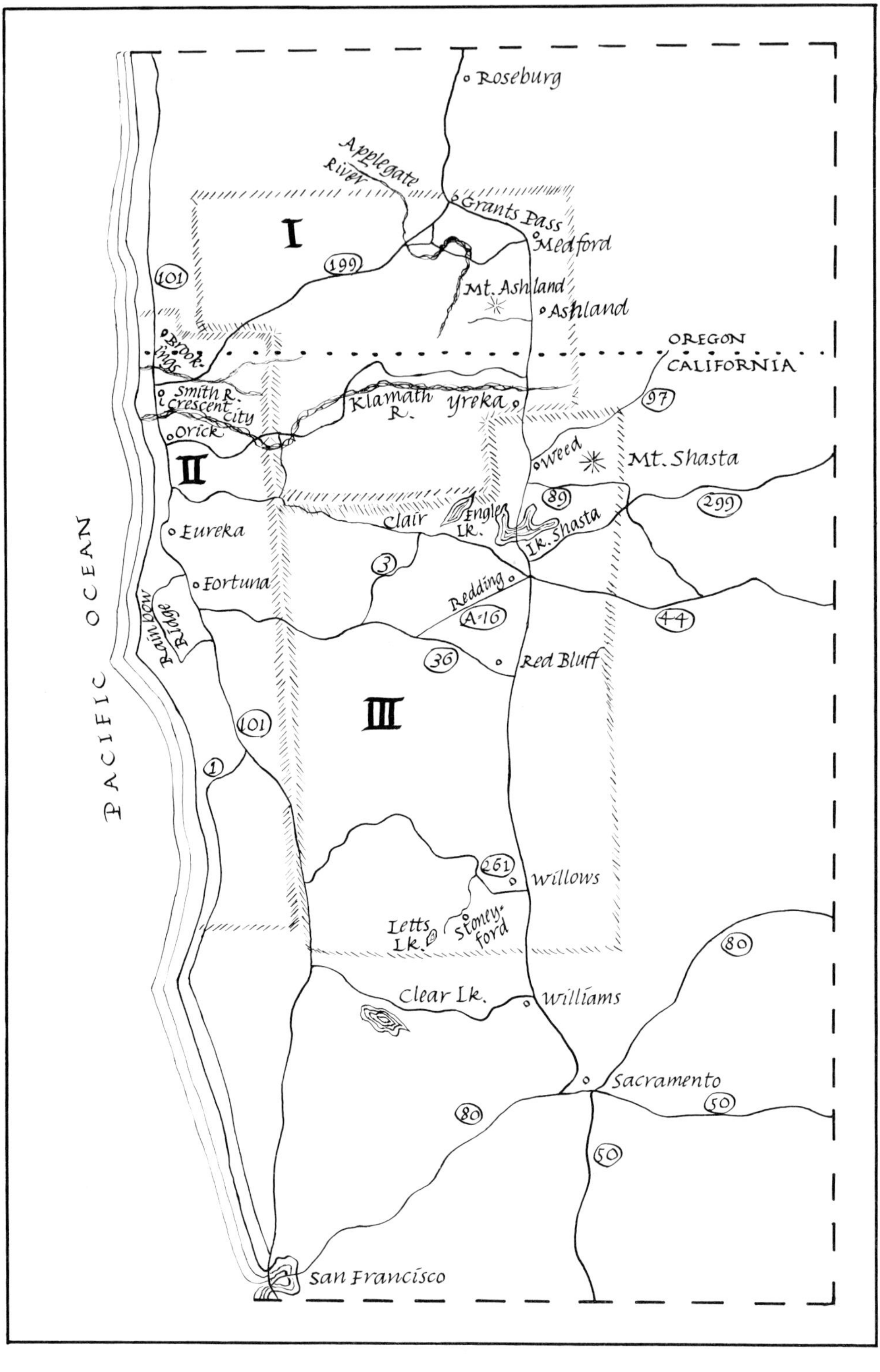

Roseburg
Applegate River
Grants Pass
Medford
I
199
101
Mt. Ashland
Ashland
Brookings
OREGON
CALIFORNIA
Smith R.
Crescent City
Klamath R.
Yreka
97
Orick
Weed
Mt. Shasta
II
89
299
Clair Engle Lk.
Lk. Shasta
Eureka
3
Fortuna
Redding
A-16
44
Rainbow Ridge
36
Red Bluff
PACIFIC OCEAN
101
III
1
261
Willows
Letts Lk.
Stoneyford
80
Clear Lk.
Williams
Sacramento
80
50
50
San Francisco

INTRODUCTION

Most trail guides are written for the serious hiker or backpacker who is willing to walk many miles over sometimes difficult terrain. This book, however, is for families with children, and for the casual hiker, who may want to enjoy the wilderness without enduring too many miles or too much rough terrain.

The Trinity Alps, Mt. Shasta, the Siskiyous, and, of course, the redwoods and the Pacific coast, all are areas accessible to a family by automobile. Such access allows you to drive through forests or along extravagantly scenic ridgetops, and to walk through coastal redwoods or beside clear, unpolluted streams. This guide will help you get to these places.

All trips included here begin on either a state or U.S. highway. Yet the trips take you away from the congestion and development along the major roads, into some of the wilder places in the mountains, valleys and the coast of northwestern California and southwestern Oregon. The drives are scenic—sometimes historic—and all are possible in a sedan. Each drive incorporates access to maintained trails. Some of these hikes are challenging, but all have been chosen as pleasant walks which often can be extended by the more hardy.

Because this guide is for those who want to enjoy the forest a day at a time, it is an extremely selective book. The 25 trips described here represent less than half of the trips taken while preparing the book. Included here are drives and hikes which offer some combination of scenery, history and either a lake, river or creek. The trips shun resort areas, housing tracts and other forms of development. There is no way to avoid logged areas, but perhaps in seeing them you will understand what is happening to the wilderness, and will help to make our exploitation of nature more responsible and a little less inevitable.

Another thing to be aware of is that our use of the forest is increasing. More people are using the forests for all sorts of recreation. One form of recreational activity involves so-called "off-the-road-vehicles." In our opinion, no motorized vehicle should be allowed off the road onto any hiking trail, for several reasons: many trails are dangerous for anything but foot traffic; most trails are damaged by the spinning and gouging of mud or dirt tires; motorized vehicles endanger pedestrians on narrow trails, especially small children; and, motorized vehicles make so much noise and so much stink that they completely destroy the sounds and fragrances which attract hikers to the trails. A proposed compromise: allow motorcycles and off-road vehicles, etc. in the forest, but restrict them to roads. Many old logging roads provide enough scenery, solitude and challenge to satisfy any biker or driver.

With the exception of forest fires, the damage caused by numbers of novice or insensitive hikers is relatively moderate. While such damage cannot be condoned, at least it can sometimes be repaired. Hopefully, increased forest usage of the right kind will contribute to a greater public awareness and understanding of the wilderness and, in turn, will protect the forest from permanent damage.

We hope that as you use this guide book to explore and enjoy the forests, you will develop some insight and opinion about our wilderness, and that you will share these thoughts with your local Forest Service personnel, as well as with your Congressmen.

History of the State of Jefferson

In 1852 a bill was introduced into the California State Legislature (then in Vallejo) to form the State of Shasta, which would include the bordering counties of California and Oregon. Proponents of the bill complained of poor military protection from hostile Indians, inadequate mail service and high taxes. The bill died in committee, but in 1853 some bay area newspapers called for the formation of the State of Klamath, to include that area from Cape Mendocino to the Umpqua River. Complaints this time called for better representation of the separate interests and unique character of this area. Nothing developed from these proposals, but the next year, on January 7, 1854, a meeting was held in Jacksonville, Oregon to plan a convention, at which representatives from the counties involved would meet to organize a new state called Jackson. Enthusiasm was dampened by politicians who feared these activities would interfere with Oregon winning statehood, and the movement was temporarily subdued by the threat of renewed Shasta Indian hostilities. In 1855 the issue was raised again, this time the primary complaint being about the bad roads in the area.

Those who wanted separate statehood during the mid 1800's were quite serious. They felt isolated and victimized, and resented their inadequate roads. For much the same reasons, although perhaps only half seriously this time, the issue of secession reappeared in 1941. On Thursday, November 27 of that year, the State of Jefferson seceded from Oregon and California. Citizens of the new "state" put up road blocks on U.S. 99 and handed out brochures, stating their intent "to secede each Thursday until further notice," which meant until they got good roads into the copper belt beween the highway and the ocean.

The exact boundaries of the State of Jefferson lie generally from the Pacific over to the high plateau in Nevada, on the other side of the Cascades and Sierra Nevada (same range, different states). The northern border was to have been north of Roseburg, Oregon near the 40th parallel, and the southern border near Redding, California, around the 44th parallel. The state capitol was Yreka, California, and the state seal was represented by a gold pan (for panning gold—not a golden pan), around which was lettered THE GREAT SEAL OF THE STATE OF JEFFERSON. Across the center of the seal were the characters "XX," indications of just how the citizenry felt about California and Oregon—Doublecrossed.

The State of Jefferson seceded in November, and on December 4, 1941, longtime activist for the new state, Judge John L. Childs, of Crescent City, California, was inaugurated acting governor, on the Yreka courthouse lawn. Newsreels were made of the activities, and news coverage of the formation of the forty-ninth state was to be released to the world on December 8. Alas, for Jefferson and the world, Japan attacked Pearl Harbor on December 7, 1941, and again the project of forming a fourth Pacific coast state was frustrated by matters of immediate concern.

The Territory of This Book

The general realm of this book is the Klamath Mountains, which are the heartland of the State of Jefferson. These ranges begin with the Siskiyous, north of the border, and end on the southern slopes of the Trinity Alps. Mt. Shasta and Interstate 5, and the Pacific Ocean, delineate the approximate eastern and western boundaries of our concern. These mountains, which involve the Klamath and Trinity River systems, comprise the second most productive gold mining area in California. The redwood forests, the mining and the ocean, the mountains, the climate and the botany have all created a unique area and economy that still encourages occasional but fervid interest in the State of Jefferson. Officials in Sacramento and Salem will not begin to understand such talk until they have at least walked and driven through these mountains, talked to the people and learned some of the history.

The area of the Trinity Alps was settled by gold miners. Narrow tracks over the mountains became pack trails, gold camps became settlements and settlements became towns. Gold brought the people to the mountains, lumber kept them there.

In 1842, English pirates discovered gold on the Trinity River at Sailors Bar and in 1849, Major Pierson Reading found gold at Big Bar. The following year rumors of gold brought a rush to the Weaver Basin and, in 1851, $100,000 in gold was found in the creeks and rivers of Weaver Basin, just one gold mining region in the Trinity Alps. Quartz and other minerals were found, but mining in general declined after the turn of the century. Smaller operations continued until a government war order in 1942 closed all gold mines. Very few persons still look for gold in these mountains, and some say that gold still can be found. Perhaps so, but as you hike along a ridge or by a creek, it may not be difficult to imagine the pack trains, the Chinese workers imported to mine gold, and the rough white miners at their sluice boxes. Chances are, though, the images will not last very long for most of the disused mines are invisible now. The mountains, rivers, forests and scenery are all still there, and may shape more memories than could the history of a hundred years.

Gold mining attracted settlers to the redwoods as well, and, as with the Trinity Alps, logging kept the people there. Logging in the redwoods is not like logging elsewhere because redwood forests are not like those of pine, fir and hardwoods. Forests of the coastal redwood (*Sequoia sempervirons*) are tall, shaded places where the climate is cool, the air moist, and the water plentiful.

In the alluvial valleys, the trees grow tall and heavy, living for five to eight centuries. Eventually, they begin to require more water than is available, or the weight of the trunk is too much for the shallow root system to support, and they topple. Out on the hillsides the redwoods grow just as old but to less dramatic size, a fact which is surprisingly apparent. "Green gold," as the coastal redwoods have been called, is native to the Pacific coast from Monterey County north to the Chetco River area in southern Oregon.

Redwoods resist fire, fungus and insects. Their regenerative powers are greater than those of any other conifer. Early settlers cleared the trees, only to find that the stumps sprouted new trees; they burned the stumps, only to find that the roots sprouted new trees. Because the wood lasts so long, it is in great demand, and so the redwoods have been logged for more than two centuries. The problem with logging is that no matter how well-managed the forest, no matter how efficient the harvest, and no matter how quick the regeneration, a forest that has been logged is not awesome or majestic.

It was not until 1901, under pressure from the Sempervirens Club, that the California legislature authorized the purchase of land for the first state redwood park. The state redwood park system grew due to continued pressure and concern from private quarters, which eventually elicited the cooperation of logging companies, who donated some parcels of old growth forest. The state eventually consented to an arrangement of matching the funds donated by private parties for the purpose of preserving the redwoods.

After the state had built a system of redwood parks, the federal government finally started listening to those concerned about the trees. In 1968 the Redwood National Park was established, adding more than 33,000 acres of redwood forest land to the state parks which are included within it. The arrangement with the state parks is tenuous, and the area is under joint management.

That there are now any huge, old redwoods left is due to public involvement. About ten percent of the redwood forest land has been set aside from logging because perceptive citizens, in only a few decades, overcame the once-popular attitude that there was enough old growth redwood timber to last forever. The thousands of acres of trees that have been saved do present some good recreation, and the adjoining coastal scenery adds even more to the experience.

Gold and then lumber—it happened that way again in the Siskiyous, along the Klamath River and north to Jacksonville. The gold rush overflowed from the south into the Siskiyous and, in 1850, John Scott found the first nugget of gold at what is now Scott Bar, near the mouth of the Scott River.

The 49'ers found gold in the Siskiyous in '50, and were soon drifting even farther north. Gold was discovered in the Rogue River Valley by two packers, James Cluggage and J. R. Poole, in December 1851. They found nuggets while camped along a tributary of the Rogue, staked their claims, and within a year saw more than a thousand more miners move into the area. By 1853 the community became the town of Jacksonville, one of few towns in the southern Oregon Territory—still an interesting place to visit.

How to Use This Book

This book is divided into three sections, each representing a general area and terrain. The sections include numbered trips, and each trip includes a drive, or drives, leading to one or more trails.

The tabular information preceding each trip gives the name of the general area of the trip, and the national forest or state park which administers the area. The mileage shown, unless specified as a loop, is the approximate one-way mileage of the trip. A general description of road conditions indicates whether the entire road is paved, and if not, about what type of road you can expect to encounter. Finally, the recommended hikes are found along the drives.

The maps are drawn approximately, not precisely, to scale. They are intended to show you what turns to take, and where to find the trailheads, using approximate distances, landmarks, road signs and bearings. If you want a more complete map of an area, check with a district ranger station. Please remember, when using either our maps or those provided by a state park or the Forest Service, that things change. Such occasional events as the moving of trailheads, abandoning sections of road and trail, the cutting of roads and trails, and the closure of access across private property will affect any map. Also, check at the local ranger station for road and trail conditions when traveling off season.

The text of each trip supplies driving and hiking directions, some idea of the characteristic scenery in the area, and often includes references to local history. Photographs have been selected to give a general idea of the area. We suggest that once you decide upon a trip, you read about the *entire* trip, glance over the map, and then use the map and trip description as you travel.

Clothing

In the mountains, the trails are rocky, the days hot, and the nights sometimes cool. On the coast, the days are cool, the nights sometimes chilly, and rain always a possibility. If extensive walking is anticipated, it may be worthwhile to include sturdy walking shoes or hiking boots, well broken in. Clothing for the mountain hikes should be cool, and for any hiking, it should be roomy and not restricting. A sweater and rain jacket or windbreaker should be packed no matter where you will be hiking. A hat and sunglasses will give added comfort on hot, bright days.

Hazards

The Klamath Mountains provide habitat for yellowjackets, ticks, scorpions and rattlesnakes, but don't let that scare you away. The forests are not crowded with these creatures. While doing all of the driving, hiking and camping required to write this book, we received only one yellowjacket sting and one tick bite between us. The only scorpions we saw were those that a local boy had caught for study. We encountered no rattlesnakes.

Yellowjackets become aggressive toward mid and late season, when they may sting without provocation. If a member of your family is allergic to bee stings, appropriate medication should be carried.

Ticks are small, hard insects which cling to the underbrush, waiting to hitch a ride on a passing mammal. Inspect yourself and your children daily for ticks, particularly around belt and cuff lines, and the tops of shoes and socks. Pay special attention to your hair. Dogs should be checked carefully, too.

There are a number of animals that can harm man, but we resist the assumption that such beasts were installed on this planet specifically to harass humans. To many animals, man is irrelevant. Except where pollution, logging and the general destruction of "progress" are concerned, many animals go for generations without considering the human as anything but an occasional curiosity, if they consider us at all. Wild animals have their lives and we have ours, until man walks into the forest. Then, the human can become invader, and when he does, the wild beasts can be expected to respond. Generally the response will be one calculated to discourage the invader. Thus, bees and yellowjackets sting, scorpions sting, and rattlesnakes strike. Of these, the latter two are both the most serious and the most infrequent.

To avoid scorpion sting and rattlesnake bite, one has only to avoid infringing upon the immediate territory of the creature. This is why most books on the subject say something like, "Be careful where you step. Don't put your hands or feet anywhere you can't look first. You probably won't find a scorpion or a rattlesnake, but if you should, walk around it and leave it alone." No great service is done to mankind by killing snakes or scorpions. In fact, a multiple disservice is done. Threatening the animal is dangerous. Killing it upsets the food chain. Removing it deprives others of the opportunity to enjoy its presence, or at least the knowledge of its existence.

Alertness, calmness, and a good first aid book and kit are important assets in the woods.

A greater hazard than getting bitten or stung is driving on unfamiliar mountain roads. These are often steep, winding and bumpy. If the curve is too tight to see around, honk the horn before taking it. Use your headlights on the back roads and watch for wildlife on the road. Another good practice, before beginning one of these trips, is to fill the gas tank, check the oil, radiator, battery and brakes, and pack extra water.

Forest Courtesy

Another sort of hazard comes in human form, and is recognized by noise, litter, damaged trees and undergrowth, and forest fires. What forests and wild places we have left are too precious to spoil. Please be careful, thoughtful, and leave the wilderness better than you found it.

Wilderness Areas and Permits

Wilderness areas are those officially designated as such by Congress. They are limited to non-motorized use, which means that no motor boats, trail bikes or other "off-the-road vehicles," and no chain saws or other power machinery, are permitted within wilderness area boundaries. Permits are required to enter most wilderness areas. The permits are free, at this time, and enable the Forest Service to know about how many people enter their wilderness each year, and through which portals.

Elsewhere in California, the wilderness permit system is already being used to limit use of particular areas. The Forest Service decides how many people an area can accommodate at a given time, and issues only that many permits. Some Forest Service personnel suspect that before too long, small fees may be charged for wilderness permits. Then the fees will be gradually increased, until it is the price of the permit which limits access to the wilderness area. It may be necessary to limit access to some fragile wilderness areas, but access should not be limited to the rich. As of now, no fees are charged for any wilderness area described in this book. Perhaps you would like to join us in the hope that no fee ever will be charged for access to trails and primitive campsites on federal land.

Acknowledgments

Our thanks to Mrs. Donna Young, of the Trinity County Historical Society, and to Mrs. John Shuford of the Shasta County Historical Society.

Our appreciation to all U.S. Forest Service personnel, with special thanks to Gus Nichols, previously of the Siskiyou National Forest; Kieth Krummer, Jim Benson and Ernest Weinberg of the Klamath National Forest; and to Charles Smay of the Mendocino National Forest. We also acknowledge help by personnel of the state redwood parks.

Our particular thanks to Brad Bleything, for hours and hours of darkroom assistance.

Finally, our sincere thanks to *Chutzpah!*, the 13-year-old Volkswagen, without which this book would not have been possible.

—DB/SEH

Potem Falls

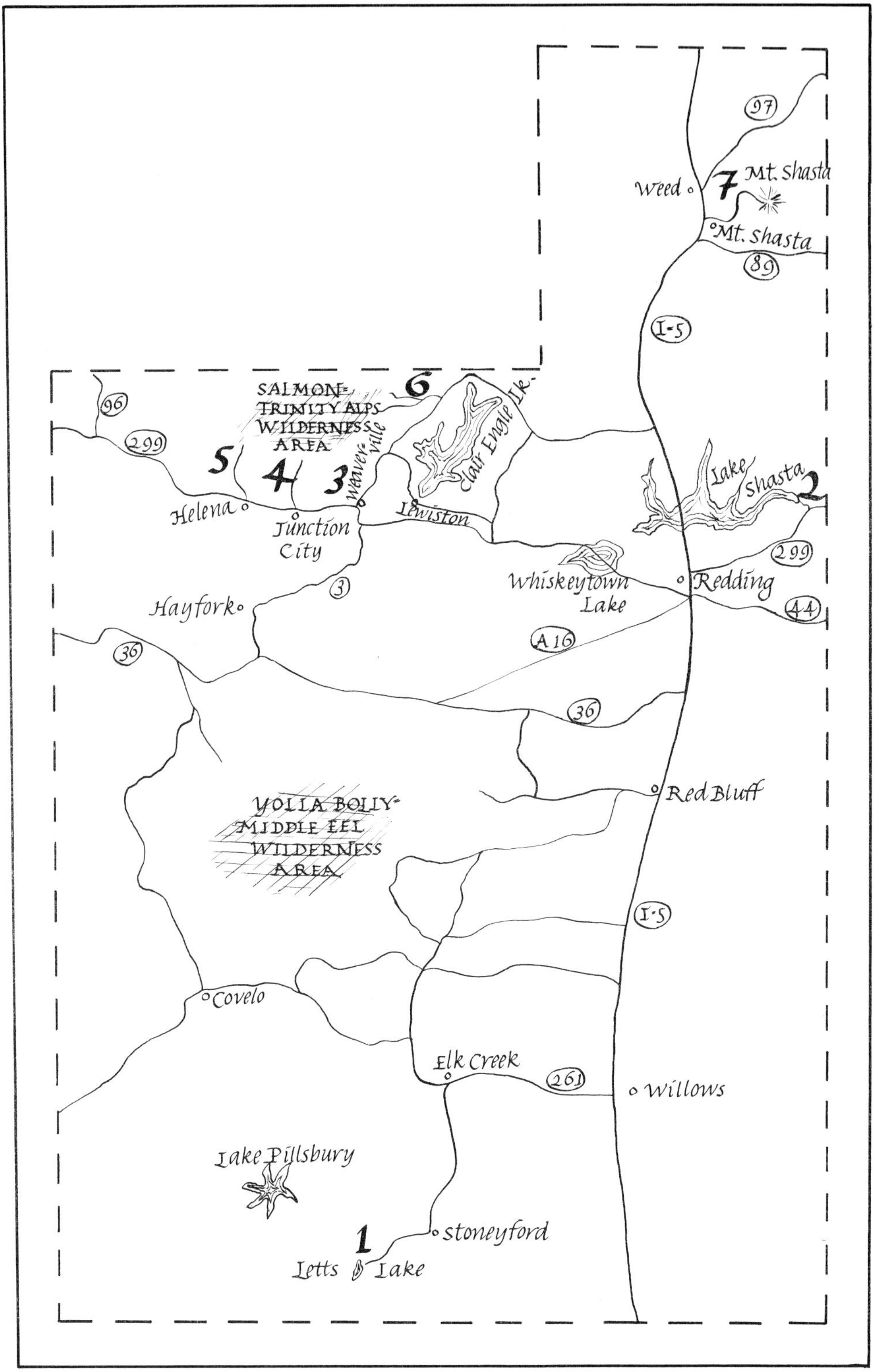
97
Weed
7
Mt. Shasta
Mt. Shasta
89
I-5
96
SALMON-TRINITY ALPS WILDERNESS AREA
6
299
5
4
3
Weaverville
Clair Engle Lk.
Lake Shasta
2
Helena
Junction City
Lewiston
299
Whiskeytown Lake
Redding
3
Hayfork
44
A16
36
36
Red Bluff
YOLLA BOLLY-MIDDLE EEL WILDERNESS AREA
I-5
Covelo
Elk Creek
261
Willows
Lake Pillsbury
1
Stoneyford
Letts Lake

I. TRINITY ALPS – MT. SHASTA

The Trinity Alps are among the best known mountains in northwestern California. The fame and popularity of these peaks must be due to their unique ruggedness. Traveling through these mountains, one sometimes finds the ridges in mist, while other days may have them detailed against a bright, clear sky. The creeks and streams are just as bright and clear, and the recent history of settlement and mining, now half-hidden by a century, was as much shaped by these mountains as was the flow of its waters.

Perhaps this beauty and popularity explains the extremes of development found in the area. Many of the trails explored, but not included in this book, are long and demanding, and withhold scenic rewards for several miles. The other extreme is exemplified by certain roads which seem to provide adequate access to an otherwise remote area. But then, at the end of the road, is a resort, complete with cabins along private river frontage! And in the midst of a national forest! Feeling that the first extreme makes the going too difficult for many families, and that the second is not worth the trouble, we have nonetheless found enough trips to give families a good idea of the beautiful country available in northwestern California.

The first two trips are actually south of the Trinity Alps. Although the drive to Letts Lake (Trip 1) is over some of the bumpiest paved and unpaved roads in this book, hundreds of people drive up there from the bay area every year to spend some time rowing and fishing about the lake, or hiking in the Snow Mountain area. While Trip 2 to Potem Falls, east of Redding, has the advantage of well-maintained highway, the Forest Service road is poorly maintained. However, local boaters seem unperturbed by this, as they take advantage of the dramatic Pit River scenery.

Once into the Trinity Alps farther north the subject changes to mountains and mining. Here, mining means gold, although some quartz has also been taken from these mountains. Gold is, in fact, the key to the history and scenery of much of the Weaver Basin, where Trips 3 through 6 begin. Canyon Creek serves as a good example of those earlier days. In its heyday, the creek was lined with saloons and the miners led such a zestful life that the area became known as "Little Bagdad." The town of Weaverville once had a population of 2,500 Chinese, brought in to work the mines. Economic pressures from the whites forced them into competitive groups called Tongs. Rivalry between Tongs became so fierce that a Tong War was fought in 1854, where the grade school now stands.

It may have been only gold which wrote such a hardy and interesting history, but it may also have been the mountains here, whose valleys are deep, whose creeks are swift and clear, and whose peaks and ridges run from north to south, standing as barrier behind barrier as you look toward the coast.

Trip 7, the last in this section, takes you onto Mt. Shasta itself. From here you may look up to the peak, or southwest to the Trinity Alps and Castle Crags. The hike on Shasta is one of the few in this book through alpine meadows. (Incidentally, hikes in Castle Crags State Park were not included in this book because there is a fee for the use of the trails. A small map brochure can be obtained from park headquarters, if you would care to pay a fee to walk upon public land.)

Most of the trips in this section take you to heights of from 4,000 to 7,000 feet. Altitudes such as these are surprisingly warm in the daytime but often cool at night. The trails are blocked with snow from middle or late fall to middle or late spring. If you travel in one of the borderline seasons, some of the roads may be unstable, so check first with a local ranger station about road and trail conditions.

1 LETTS LAKE

Mendocino National Forest

Drive: 39 miles from Willows

Road: Partly paved; mostly gravel in fair to poor condition

Hike: Letts Lake Trail

Features: Picnicking, camping, lake access, vehicle control area

Letts Lake is a small, warm, stream-fed, man-made lake, stocked with trout, and surrounded on three sides with small campgrounds and picnic areas. Motor boats are not allowed on the lake, which is near the boundary of the Snow Mountain Vehicle Control Area. While Letts Lake can provide some solitude and recreation during the week, it is popular on summer weekends.

Take the Willows exit from Interstate 5, following the signs to Elk Creek and then to Stonyford (pop. 220), or from the Maxwell exit at I-5, drive generally northeast through Sites and Lodoga. The road is better through Elk Creek.

From Stonyford, take the signed road angling off to the east. The bumpy, paved road climbs up, curving, and soon becomes dirt and gravel. A few miles later you will pass through the Letts Valley Timber Sale, which was cut between 1955 and 1958. The drive is remarkable for the subtle strength of the graceful mountains. At the end of the drive, Letts Lake offers solace from the summer heat.

Letts Lake Trail

The trail around the lake is about 1½ miles long. During the circuit you will see frogs among the cattails and, in the warm water near shore, some very large tadpoles.

The Snow Mountain Vehicle Control Area stops short of being a designated wilderness area. Because the area is already roadless and restricted, the Forest Service is concentrating on other areas, presently roaded and unrestricted, where conditions merit the official expense and designation of wilderness area. We had hoped to take you by car to the boundary of this area, and then by trail in toward Snow Mountain. However, the maze of roads is so poorly signed that it is difficult to find the trail, and in such poor condition that we couldn't recommend sedans going there anyhow. The area could be worthwhile, however, so if you do want to explore it, ask at the district ranger's office at Stonyford if the roads have been signed and improved.

Letts Lake

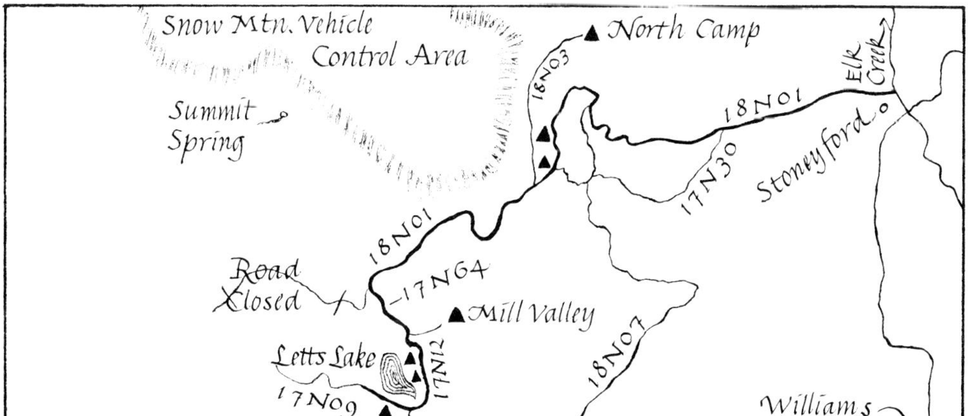
Snow Mtn. Vehicle
Control Area
North Camp
Summit
Spring
18N03
Elk
Creek
18N01
Stoneyford
17N30
18N01
Road
Closed
17N64
Mill Valley
Letts Lake
17N12
18N07
17N09
17N14
Williams
I-5

2 POTEM FALLS

Shasta-Trinity National Forest

Drive: 40 miles from Redding

Road: Some paved; some dirt, in good to poor condition

Hike: Potem Falls Trail

Features: Picnicking, primitive camping, stream and reservoir access

For much of this trip you will drive along Cedar Creek, often surrounded by ranch and farm country—fields with grazing cows and horses, or acres and acres of rocky grassland supporting occasional oak and pine. Then you will drive up into the mountains, to a reservoir and falls.

Just out of Redding on California 299E a sign reads: "Old Oregon Trail, Shasta College." The college is built right on what purports to be the Old Oregon Trail, which continued on to Shasta. The trail crosses Highway 299E below the college, then crosses California 44, 6 miles below Redding near Cedar Creek.

Those intrigued by ruins can observe the abandoned Afterthought Mine just past Ingot. Started by the Afterthought Mining Company in 1904, the mine produced copper until 1908. A wooden bridge, now partially destroyed, once crossed Cedar Creek and serviced the mine. While you can no longer get across to the mine, most of the wooden construction is still visible, including the several hundred foot covered water trough.

Two miles past the town of Round Mountain, a sign on the left indicates "Pit River, 9 miles." Turn here and continue along a dirt road. When you reach a fork, continue straight ahead to Fender's Flat Bridge. If you turn right at the fork, the road leads to a primitive camping area beside a reservoir. Here you will find a boat launch, a deep, wide pool of water and a large meadow which provides picnicking and primitive camping.

Beyond the bridge it is about a mile to a small sign on your left indicating Potem Falls. If you arrive at a fork in the road, you've driven too far.

Potem Falls Trail

The short trail down to the falls is steep and gravelly, so use caution on the descent. The falls is created by a creek which funnels through a narrow rock formation and plunges 30 feet into a deep, emerald green basin. Fir and interior live oak provide shade for grassy areas on which to picnic near the road above the falls.

Afterthought Mine

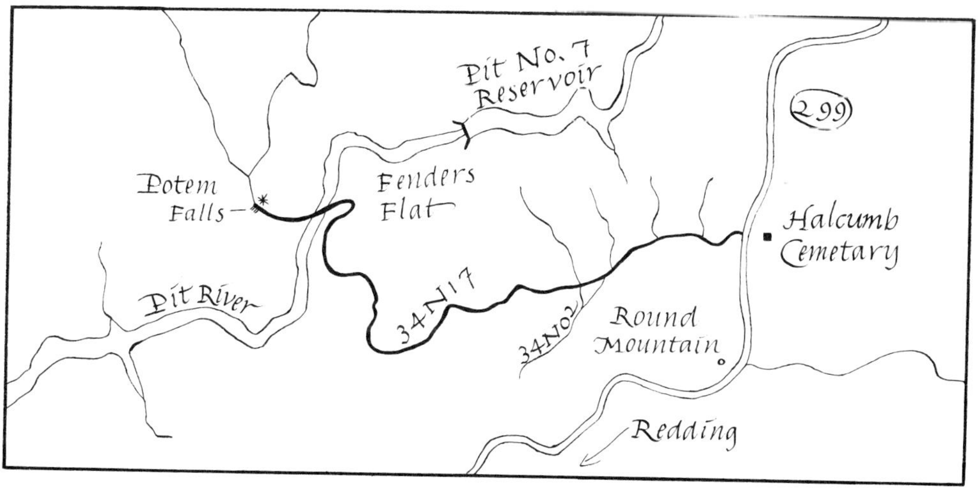

3 GARDEN GULCH—EAST WEAVER LAKE

Shasta-Trinity National Forest

Drive: 25-mile loop from Weaverville

Road: Gravel, in fair condition but slow driving

Hike: East Weaver Lake Trail

Features: Picnicking, camping, mountain lake and creek access

A trip in Weaver Basin is as historic as it is scenic. On this drive you will rise through the forest, walk over a ridge and look, or walk, down through a high meadow to East Weaver Lake. The name Weaver, which is repeated several times in naming the natural features of the area, comes from John Weaver, a miner, businessman and later a Confederate officer. He settled Weaverville, and along with Daniel Bennett and James Howe, built the first cabin there. Each man wanted the settlement named for himself, but John Weaver won at a drawing of pine needles, which gave the town his name.

Just west of Weaverville, a paved road leads north from California 299, past the high school, onto a gravel road. While unsigned, this is USFS 33T138, a shady road to Weaver-Bally Mountain and Lookout. Take the road to the left at the first junction but notice the other road, as you may want to follow it on the way back. From the road to Weaver-Bally, you can look back over the forest to Weaverville. On long, straight grades, beware of shallow ditches put into the road, to drain water from the roadbed. The trailhead is on the right. Drive 2 miles past the trailhead to the lookout, or just a few hundred yards past it to a safe turnaround, and come back to the signed trail.

East Weaver Lake Trail

The trail is steep toward the top of the ridge, but it is not as difficult as it may appear. Walk up, past bushes smelling of camphor, and plants smelling of mint. Follow the trail to the left, for a view of the lake from the ridge. Contour around behind the lake, dropping gently out onto the rocky meadow where the trail is marked by stacks of three stones each. If your family enjoys short backpacks, consider East Weaver Lake as a possible campsite.

On the drive back, enjoy a slight side trip along the road, left, to East Weaver Creek. Take care, though, as there are one or two surprise drops along this narrow dirt road. Drive through the creek (slowly and steadily), and then arrive at East Weaver Campground. Both the creek ford and the campground are suitable picnic spots. The pavement resumes beyond the campground and leads through Five Cent Gulch to Weaverville.

Near the grade school in Five Cent Gulch is the site of the 1854 Tong War. Due to the socio-economic pressures of competing with white miners on foreign soil, the Chinese miners joined together in Tongs. Four Tongs were involved in this war—3 Tongs called "Canton men," or composed of those who came from Canton, opposed a Tong of men from Hong Kong, called the "Yong-wa Company." The fight was over a gambling debt between the Yong-wa Company and the Canton men. The Chinese were not allowed firearms, so the weaponry consisted of such implements as locally-forged tridents mounted on long poles. Some of these weapons can be seen at the excellent historical museum in Weaverville.

White miners surrounded the battlefield to watch the skirmish and bet on the outcome. One of these men fired into the crowd of Chinese to get things started, and was later tallied as the only white man to be among the few people killed that day. The battle ended as the Yong-wa Company forced the other three Tongs from the field. A man from each side continued fighting until one was killed. His opponent died of his wounds within two weeks. Such was life around Weaverville just 125 years ago.

East Weaver Lake

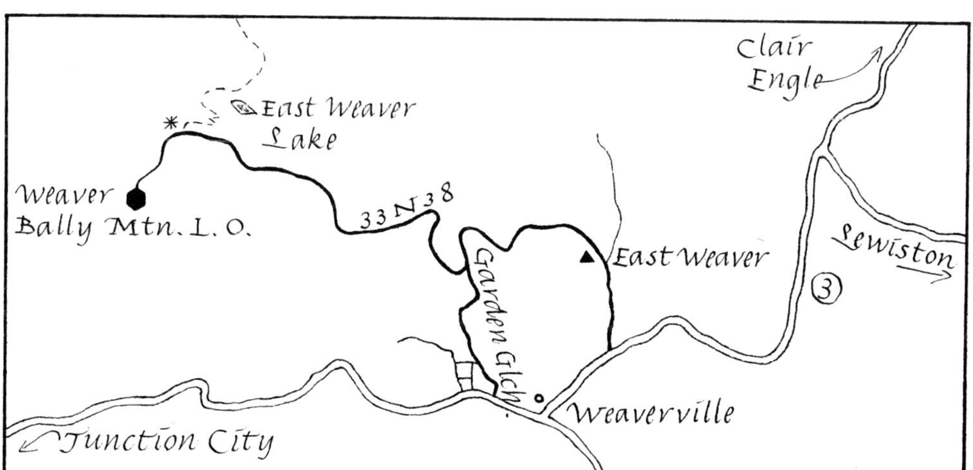

4 CANYON CREEK

Shasta-Trinity National Forest

Drive: 21 miles from Weaverville

Road: Paved to within one-half mile of trailhead

Hike: Canyon Creek Trail

Features: Picnicking, camping, wilderness area

The Canyon Creek trip is remarkable for its history of mining, and the life of the miners who worked the creek. If you would care to walk more than 6 miles, this trip will also take you into the Salmon-Trinity Primitive Area. A wilderness permit should be obtained from the ranger station in Weaverville if you are going into the primitive area. Otherwise, you can enjoy a scenic drive and hike through these historic areas.

Take California 299 west out of Weaverville, and drive about 8 miles to Junction City (pop. 121). On this stretch of highway is a California Landmark which designates the area used as the LaGrange Mine. Claims in this area were first worked in about 1862. Thirty years later the LaGrange Hydraulic Gold Mining Company bought the claims, and brought in water over a 29-mile man-made system to sluice out the gold. According to the marker, more than 100,000,000 yards of gravel were displaced, to find some $3,500,000 worth of gold, before major operations were shut down in 1918.

At Junction City, turn sharply to the right off Highway 299 onto Canyon Creek Road. If you cross a bridge, you've driven too far. The drive along Canyon Creek is shady and scenic, and the tailings (mounds of rock and gravel) are reminders of earlier mining activity. Quartz mining was started in the late 1800's but didn't reach a peak until the early 1900's. By 1904 six saloons lined the creek, a large number for such a small area. Today, trout fishing provides most of the recreation along Canyon Creek.

Canyon Creek Trail

The road is paved all the way to Ripstein Campground, and the trailhead is but a short distance from there. Park in either of two areas, and walk to the sign which indicates the trailhead.

The primitive area boundary is 3 miles. After one-fourth mile you will find a fine view of Bear Creek, as well as access to it. The trail then leaves Bear Creek and follows above Canyon Creek for 1¾ miles, before switching back to the right. A now overgrown trail once forked from here to the left. At this point you've walked 2 miles, and the primitive area boundary is yet another mile ahead.

Open spaces along the trail reveal the large granite mountains of the Trinity Alps. The country changes along the hike. At first it is a dry, rocky terrain, relatively free of underbrush, with a forest of oak, live oak and madrone. The vegetation changes along the way to increasingly greener scenery with fir, large cedar and dense undergrowth. With such elements as the forest, river and views it is not necessary to walk as far as the primitive area boundary to enjoy this trail.

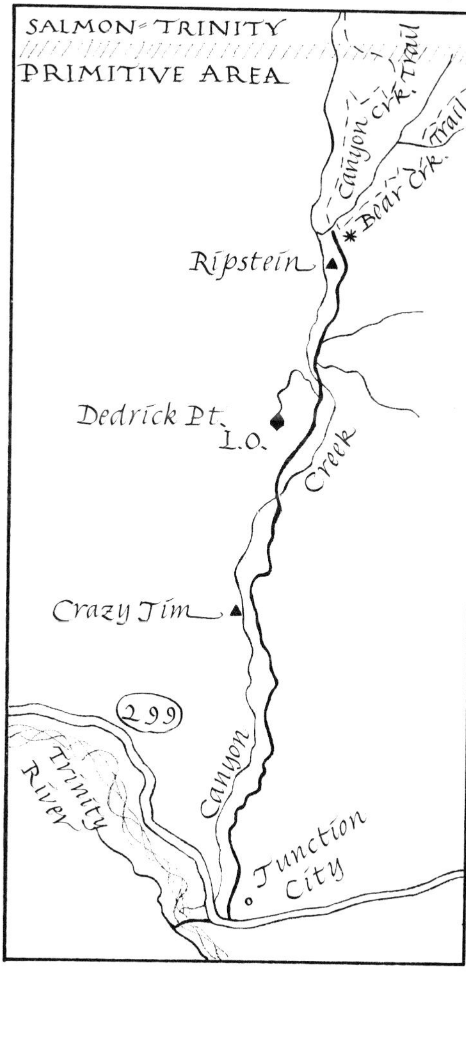

Canyon Creek Trail

5 NORTH FORK TRINITY RIVER

Shasta-Trinity National Forest

Drive: 30 miles from Weaverville

Road: Some paved; mostly gravel, in fair to poor condition

Hikes: North Fork and Whites Creek Trails

Features: Picnicking, camping, primitive area, stream access

This cool, shady drive and hike to several streams begins on California 299, several miles west of Weaverville. First, get a wilderness permit at the ranger station in Weaverville or Big Bar.

Turn off Highway 299 onto the only road north through Helena (Hel-ee-na), pop. 84. The area was settled in 1849 by French Canadian prospectors, one of whom indeed found gold up the North Fork. Mining operations grew. In 1852, the town attracted a hotel/boarding house, as well as two German families: the Meckel brothers, who established the North Fork Brewery; and the Schlomers, who came to own most of the orchards in the valley. It is believed that the economy of the area peaked in 1855 when there were over 200 acres in fruit orchard. Some of the old trees and a few of the brick buildings are all that remain of an area where life was once so wild that people called it "The Cove," and "The Bagdad of the Frontier."

Once through Helena, or North Fork as some still call it, turn right across a bridge, following the sign to Hobo Gulch and the Salmon-Trinity Primitive Area. The road surface changes from blacktop to gravel, and then you will soon come to a junction. Take the left fork, along a shady road to the campground. The road climbs and curves to the summit and the sideroad to the Backbone Ridge Lookout. It is a bumpy mile up, but the view is worth it, and the "helispot" up there might be in operation. From the lookout junction, the road drops 5 miles to Hobo Gulch Campground, ahead and down, and the trailhead, off to the right. The parking area is near the horse camp, with its wooden ramp for leading horses to and from their conveyances.

North Fork and Whites Creek Trails

The North Fork and Whites Creek Trails lead into the Salmon-Trinity Primitive Area, where ALL MOTORIZED VEHICLES ARE PROHIBITED, and permits are required.

Along the trail, just past Keystone Flat, cross Backbone Creek and follow the metal sign, indicating the "Highwater Trail" uphill to a junction of three trails. The trail to the right leads 3 miles along Backbone Creek, ending at Baker's Cabin. The trail to the left drops to the North Fork of the Trinity River. Here, you will find a gravel beach and bar, with some good wading.

The middle trail leads uphill to another junction. The trail to the left from this junction is the Whites Creek Trail, bordering that creek approximately 2 miles to Bear Wallow Meadows and beyond. The trail to the right goes north for several miles, and is still the North Fork Trail, following the North Fork Trinity River. Since the walk to this last fork and back out is some 2½ miles, we can suggest no specific destination which is within easy range. However, the several alternatives described, and the places where the family can play along the creek, are reasons enough for recommending this trail.

Backbone Creek

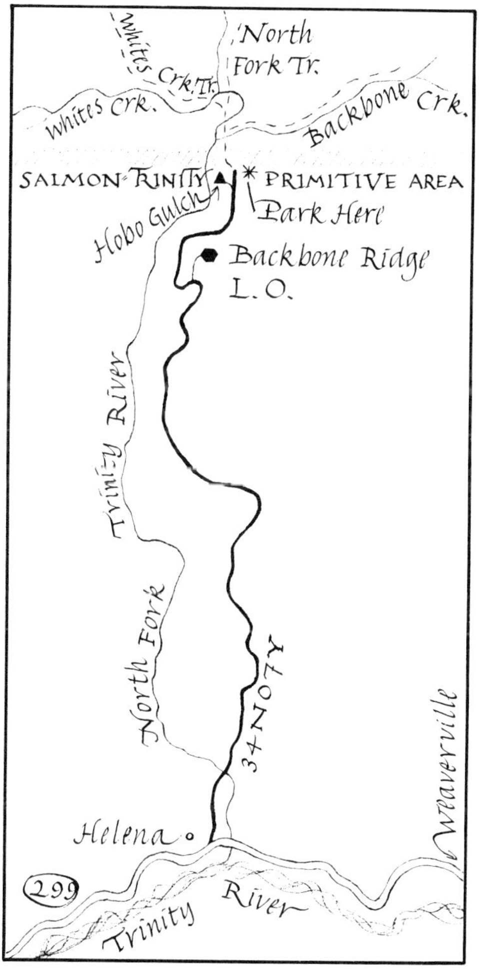

6 LAKE ELEANOR—SWIFT CREEK TRAIL

Shasta-Trinity National Forest

Drive: 85 miles round trip from Weaverville

Road: Mostly paved; some gravel, in fair to poor condition

Hikes: Lake Eleanor Trail, Swift Creek Trail

Features: Picnicking, primitive area, lake and creek access

Whether your family enjoys a secluded, quiet lake for fishing or the more strenuous activity of hiking, this trip will fill your needs. Whichever you prefer, remember to obtain a wilderness permit at the Weaverville District Ranger Station.

Take California 3 north out of Weaverville. The first part of the drive is through the mountains of Weaver Basin, while farther north the terrain changes to the pine forests and red earth typical of the Shasta Lakes. You will pass near Clair Engle Lake, on the right, before leaving Highway 3. Drive 28 miles and just past Trinity Center, cross a bridge and turn left. The sign indicates that Swift Creek Trail is 7 miles and Lake Eleanor is 8 miles. One mile in, at a signed fork, bear right to the Lake Eleanor Trail. As you drive up towards the trailhead, notice Clair Engle Lake to the east.

Lake Eleanor Trail

A small parking area is situated near a Forest Service sign board. The road uphill leads to the trail. The road to the left is used for logging.

Walk uphill where a sign on the left indicates the Salmon-Trinity Primitive Area Boundary. Once on this sometimes rocky trail, keep right and continue for one-quarter mile, and then cross a road and resume the trail on the other side. This is the same road on which you entered; however, we do not advise driving to this point as the road is privately owned and may be closed by a gate at any time.

The trail continues on a slight upgrade for one-half mile to the lake. A pathway around to the opposite end of the lake offers several spots where one may get to the water. Lake Eleanor (elev. 4,950 feet) is a small, spring-fed lake. It covers 2 acres, is 29 feet deep, and contains brook trout. Ecologically, the lake is slowly becoming a marsh. Reeds and swamp grass are beginning to reclaim areas of the lake, and lily pads are thick on portions of the surface. Truly, this is a lovely, quiet spot surrounded by firs. At the far end of the lake is a meadow along the creek which feeds the lake. Here, cobra lilies and other wildflowers mingle with the tall grass. Several places are inviting picnic spots.

Swift Creek Trail

If you would care to continue on to Swift Creek, retrace your drive to that initial, signed fork. Turn right and stay left on this well-traveled dirt road. Make a final left turn down to the trailhead and parking area.

This trail is mostly level, and has the advantage of closely following Swift Creek. You can hear the constant rush of water as the creek passes through narrow stone walls and splashes heavily over the rocks. Several places along the trail provide access to the water. After 1 mile, you reach a fork in the trail. Granite Lake is 4 miles to the left and Twin Lakes Trail is 3 miles to the right. Turn left, and in one-fourth mile arrive at a new bridge which crosses Swift Creek. The trail continues on the other side along Granite Creek. By the bridge there is ample room for picnicking or splashing in the water, or just plain resting in the shade.

After you leave the parking area for the return trip, a sign on the left indicates Lake Eleanor, 3 miles. This is some kind of connecting road, but we found it rough and unnavigable due to inadequate signing.

NO SMOKING
EXCEPT
In Cleared Areas 3 Feet in Diameter

Trail sign

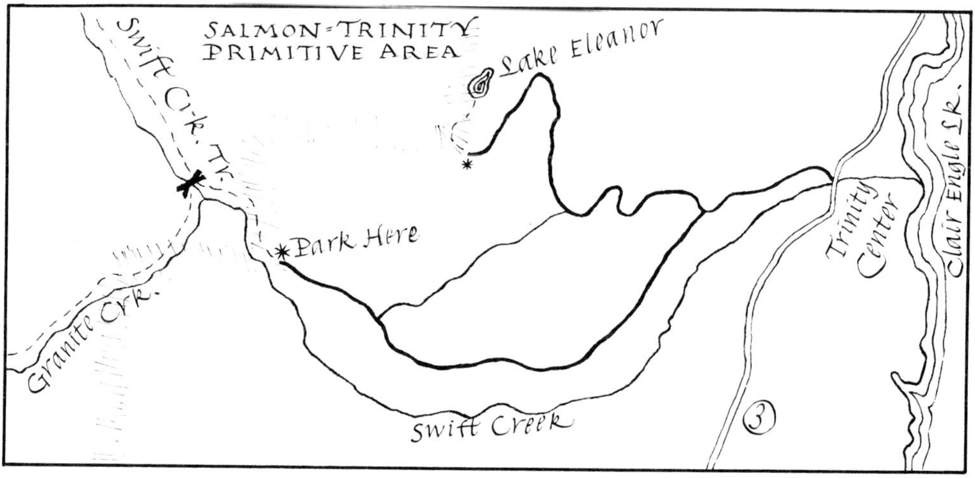
SALMON-TRINITY
PRIMITIVE AREA
Lake Eleanor
Swift Crk. Tr.
Park Here
Granite Crk.
Swift Creek
Trinity Center
Clair Engle Lk.
3

7 MT. SHASTA

Shasta-Trinity National Forest

Drive: 14 miles from the community of Mt. Shasta.

Road: Paved

Hike: Grey Butte Trail

Features: Picnicking, camping, alpine meadow

This trip allows a much closer look at Mt. Shasta than you would get just passing by on the freeway. Grey Butte Trail offers a convenient way to walk through an alpine meadow below the south face of the 14,162-foot "friendly giant."

Take the Mt. Shasta Ski Bowl exit off I-5 and follow the signs to the ski bowl. Once through the small community of Mt. Shasta, the drive leads through an area reforested with ponderosa pine. When these trees reach adequate maturity, this once vacant area will be used by the Forest Service for logging and recreation.

The highway soon winds through stands of subalpine fir, although Mt. Shasta is in prominent view most of the time. As you are gaining more than 7,000 feet in elevation, notice the view to the southwest, which includes Castle Crags and the Salmon-Trinity Alps.

Grey Butte Trail

A sign on the right indicates Panther Meadow Campground. Turn here and go to the far end of the campground where the Grey Butte Trail begins at a sign in the meadow. Walk on a slight upgrade, following a stream. Wildflowers are abundant, particularly the vermillion-colored Indian paintbrush and the low, bushy alpine heather. After a short distance, enter a small stand of subalpine fir. Continue to follow the stream, then re-enter a larger, grassy meadow. At the top of the meadow, the trail dims, so you may stop here for a picnic or bushwhack your way to the top of Grey Butte (8,119 feet).

If you decide not to take the trail, drive past the campground to the ski bowl parking lot. The view from here is delightful and Mt. Shasta rises to the north.

Mt. Shasta is the subject of a number of Indian legends, as it probably had a part in the mythology of every tribe that could see it. One story from the Modocs explains how the grizzly bear came to walk on four feet instead of two.

Long ago, the Chief Sky Spirit was uncomfortable with his home in the sky. He bored a hole in the sky with a stone and pushed ice and snow from his dwelling through the hole. The resultant huge mound on the Earth is what the white man calls Mt. Shasta. Sky Spirit came down the mountain, and as he went he created trees and rivers, beaver, otter and fish, grizzly bear, and later, birds. The grizzlies then walked on two legs, and were so ferocious that Sky Spirit made them leave the mountain to live in the forest below.

Sky Spirit brought his family to live in the mountain, hollowing out the inside and making a smoke hole in the top. Sparks flew from the mountain and the earth shook whenever he threw a big log on the fire. One cold winter the wind blew so hard that the Sky Spirit sent his daughter to the top to ask the Wind Spirit to take it easy, lest the mountain blow over. This she did, being careful not to be blown away. After talking to Wind Spirit the daughter started down, then returned to look at the ocean, which her father had created since she had moved into the mountain. She incautiously put her head out of the mountain and was blown down to the forest edge.

The grizzly bears found her and raised her with their cubs. When she was grown she married the bear's eldest son and bore several children. These offspring were the first Indians. Later, as the bear mother was dying, she notified Sky Spirit that the bears had raised his daughter. Sky Spirit was delighted to find his daughter alive, but became very angry when he learned that a new race had been created without his doing. He was so angry that he carried his daughter back home and declared that from then on, all grizzly bears would have to walk with their heads down.

Grey Butte Trail

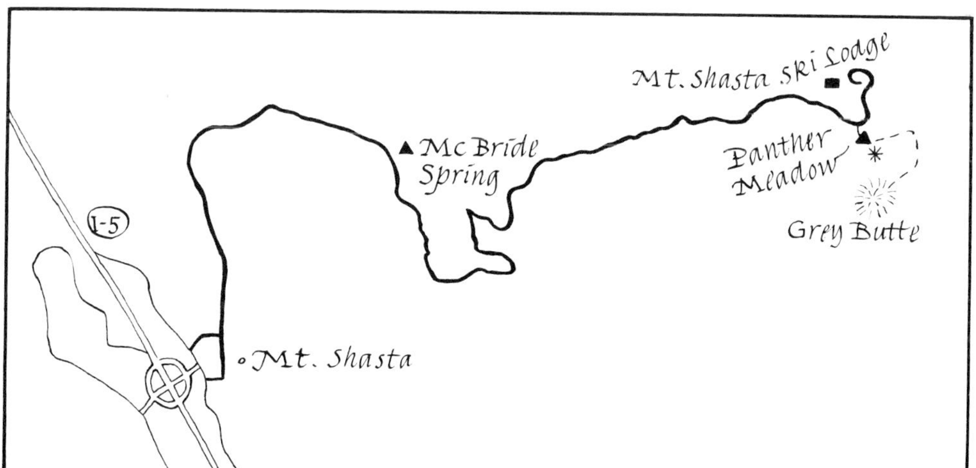

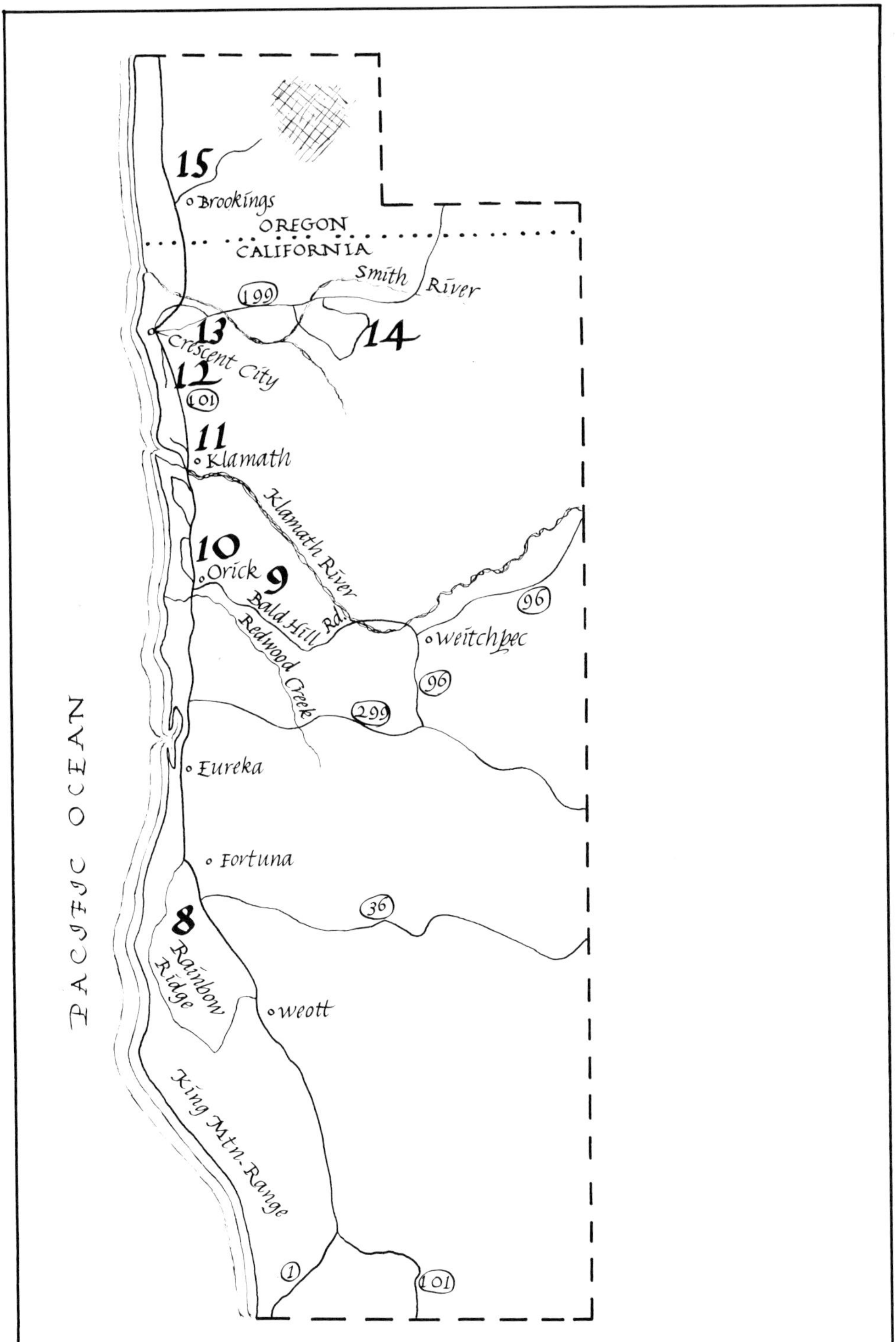
15
Brookings
OREGON
CALIFORNIA
Smith River
199
13
14
Crescent City
12
101
11
Klamath
Klamath River
10
Orick
9
Bald Hill Rd.
Redwood Creek
96
Weitchpec
96
299
PACIFIC OCEAN
Eureka
Fortuna
36
8
Rainbow Ridge
Weott
King Mtn. Range
1
101

II. THE REDWOODS AND THE COAST

Coastal redwood trees, *Sequoia sempervirons,* are considered the world's tallest species of tree. In the valleys, they grow to the dimensions which have made them famous, while on the hillsides, trees over a hundred years old may be only half the diameter and a third the height of a tree of equal age growing on the flats.

A day spent walking through a forest of noble old redwoods is a day that will be remembered for a long time. Unless you pick your spot carefully, however, you may remember the experience for all of the wrong reasons. The redwoods are being logged. The tall, old growth along the basins has been reserved, but much of it is merely a veneer—a strip of giant growth along Highway 101—in which are campgrounds, through which run trails and roads, and behind which are private homes. A number of the trails are within earshot of 101, and these we have avoided. Driving through the area, it is difficult to ignore the log trucks, loaded with large redwood logs.

Yet, thousands of acres of the trees have been set aside. About ten percent of the 2½ million acres of economically valuable redwood forest has been reserved from logging, which means that ninety percent of the redwoods have been, are being or will be logged. Those areas set aside are often named as groves, usually dedicated to people who helped save them. It is these groves that comprise the several small state redwood parks. You can still find places for a memorable walk through the redwoods, or other areas where a drive and hike can be enjoyed, away from the dwindling giants.

Among the latter is the first trip, over Rainbow Ridge (Trip 8). Most of the drive is involved with scenes of the land as it drops from mountains, through hills, to the Pacific. Trip 9, out Bald Hill Road from Crescent City, leads to two trails: the Redwood Creek Trail is longer, while the shorter trail takes you through old growth redwoods to the Lady Bird Johnson Memorial Grove.

Next, Trip 10 goes out Davison Road to Gold Bluffs Beach and Fern Canyon, where you will find some old stumps, some young redwoods and the ocean. One of the few long trails through old growth timber stretches from 101 to this beach.

Trip 11 is in the Redwood National Park. The Coastal Drive and Coastal Trail give more of the northern coastal scenery, the best of which is found along the trail. Another pair of walks within view of the Pacific is in Trip 12. Here, walking along abandoned Route 1, one gets a feel for how it used to be to travel along the coast, winding along the cliffside and getting occasional glimpses of the surf through the dense forest. Howland Hill Road, Trip 13, is another old road, and it goes up into hills where there are two trails through old forest.

The Smith River, Trip 14, is the only trip in the Six Rivers National Forest which we found suitable for family hiking. When we talked to the Forest Service personnel about trails and drives in their rugged forest, they made a few suggestions and then talked about logging. Nonetheless, there is one good drive, a good hike and a small lake to boot.

The final trip in this section is along the North Bank Road (Trip 15) out of Brookings, Oregon. The Kalmiopsis Wilderness Area in the Siskiyou National Forest is unique for its climate and botany, and this trip reveals that uniqueness, as well as a lake, some streams, and the northern natural limit of the original redwood forests.

Most of this entire section is near sea level, or just a few hundred feet above it. While snow could be a problem on the Smith River Trip, rain will be the bugaboo for most off-season travel in the redwood parks and along the coast. In fact, rain should be allowed for even during the tourist season.

8 RAINBOW RIDGE DRIVE

Humboldt Redwoods State Park

Drive: 74 miles semi-loop from Eureka

Road: Mostly paved

Hikes: Along the beach

Features: Picnicking, camping, ocean access

This drive is the most scenic, the most varied and the longest of all the drives included in the redwoods. The trip is nearly 74 miles, although this is moderated by the fact that the semi-loop drive both begins and ends on 101. The drive will take time. We suggest leaving mid-morning, taking a picnic lunch and getting back by dinner. You could, however, still enjoy the drive by making a full afternoon of it. We do not recommend hauling a mobile home on the winding, hilly roads of this drive.

In Fortuna, about 14 miles south of Eureka, take the Fernbridge exit off 101. Go through Fernbridge, a small dairy town, and cross the Eel River toward Ferndale. Ferndale is another old, small farm town now being revitalized. Many of the Victorian "carpenter's gothic" houses have been repaired and brightly painted. Some old shops have been turned into studios, galleries and boutiques, and a live theatre is active here.

The old, new town of Ferndale may itself be the destination of the drive. Should you venture farther than the scenic turnouts in the hills just beyond the town, you will soon be among the hillside pastures of Rainbow Ridge. Hillside pastures may not sound like much, but these are rugged, while the road is winding and sometimes steep. Livestock, especially sheep, graze these pastures and in spring the young lambs sometimes seem to pose shyly for the few who pass by. Frequently there are broad views of the Pacific and east, into the mountains of the Six Rivers National Forest.

Great old barns are an important part of the scenery. The good material in these structures is well preserved. None of these weathered buildings has dilapidated to the point of being abandoned. Yet they are so much a part of the hillsides that they may scarcely be noticed, as the road descends to cross a small creek and the view continually improves. Notice, also, on this descent, that there are no fences along this part of the drive. Livestock may be on the road, so keep a sharp eye while taking the curves.

The road climbs again, now through coastal underbrush, and tops out in pastures and ranches. Then drops down again, with even better ocean scenes, to where an immense pasture nearly meets the surf, and livestock may be silhouetted against the deep colors of the ocean.

Walk Along the Beach

Next comes a long drive along the beach, with the road nearly in the sand. Some, perhaps most, of this beach is private property, but the view is there for all. Several points allow public access to this lightly-used stretch of coast.

After leaving the beach, cross the Mattole River and pass through the quiet farm town of Petrolia, one of the more interesting features of which is the huge eucalyptus trees along the road. Cross Conklin Creek, and follow along the Mattole River Valley for several miles, passing the A. W. Way County Park, where you can stop for a picnic if you didn't manage it at the coast. Farther along is the small settlement of Honeydew—a post office and general store. As the road climbs from Honeydew, look back for a good view of the King Mountain Range and King Peak (4,087 feet).

The drive continues high in the mountains through forests of fir, madrone and tanoak. The road then begins to drop toward 101, into the Humboldt Redwoods

State Park, a narrow strip of large, old growth. Bull Flats Road leads through the park. On the way you will pass the Cunoe group horse camp, an old orchard and meadow with tables and stone stoves which makes a good picnic site when not being used by the equestrians. Farther down Bull Flats Road is the Pioneer Cemetery, an early morning habitat of some blacktail deer. Here, the oldest marked grave was installed in 1926. Most of the graves in this rustically-fenced yard are strewn with brightly colored plastic flowers. The last place of interest is the Albee Creek Campground which, when open in the summer, gives access to the Bull Creek Flats Trail, following Bull Creek for 5 miles.

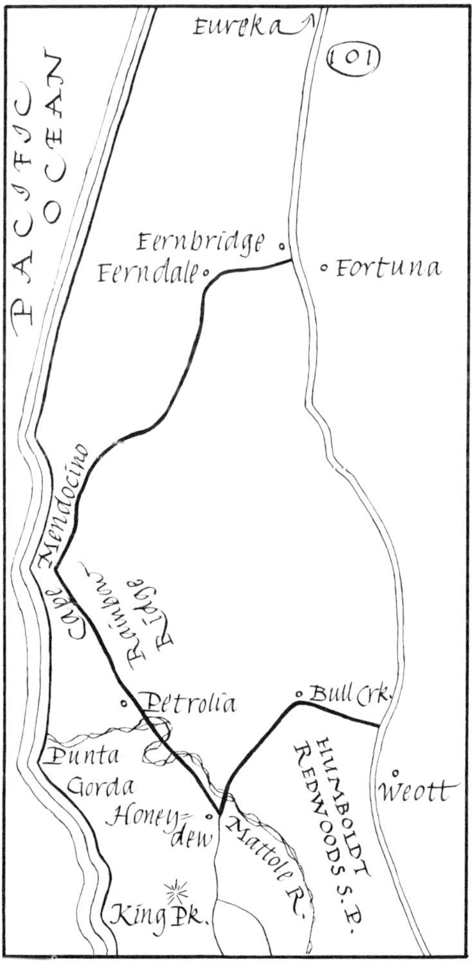

View from Rainbow Ridge

9 BALD HILL ROAD

Redwood National Park

Drive: 3 miles from Orick

Road: Paved

Hikes: Redwood Creek Trail, Lady Bird Johnson Memorial Grove Trail

Features: Picnicking, backpacker camping, creek access, redwoods

The old growth coastal redwoods along this trip are sometimes massive as in the Lady Bird Johnson Memorial Grove, or may merely be tall and mature, but smaller, as along Redwood Creek. Such factors as terrain, soil, water and climate affect these great plants so dramatically that trees growing in optimum conditions may be two or three times the bulk of those found in less favorable sites, even though both may be approximately the same age. To find these trees and their varying and pleasant surroundings, take U.S. 101 to just north of Orick. From there follow Bald Hill Road as it breaks east from Highway 101. The road ultimately leads over increasingly rough terrain some 25 miles to the Bald Hills and the small lumber town of Weitchpec. Bald Hill Road can be a rewarding departure from Highway 101, even after the pavement ends, although we refer to it here only as an access road to these two trails, both beginning about 2 miles off U.S. 101.

Redwood Creek Trail

The first trail to appear on Bald Hill Road is the Redwood Creek Trail, at the head of which is a large parking area. The trail is maintained for about 8 miles, and is broken into shorter sections. Some may be content to walk just the first few sections, either 1½ miles to the footbridge across Redwood Creek, or another one quarter mile to McArthur Creek, or a total of 2¾ miles to Elam Creek. Picnicking and play are two features of this trail. The footbridge is taken down during periods of high water, but the first section of the trail alone gives access to large, grassy meadows and the creekside.

This trail approximates the old route across the creek from Trinidad, on the coast, to Orleans, which is still a town up in the mountains behind Weitchpec. The original pack trail to the gold fields was used from 1860 to 1920.

Lady Bird Johnson Memorial Grove Trail

A trail of more recent historic interest can be found a short distance beyond the Redwood Creek Trail. Up the steep road into the hills is a view of the Pacific. Here, a paved parking area services the Lady Bird Johnson Memorial Grove Trail. The redwood grove is significant politically because it was here that President Richard M. Nixon, in 1969, signed a document commemorating this stand of ancient trees to the wife of the late President Lyndon B. Johnson.

The half-mile walk is easy and pleasant. Just beyond the grove the trail crosses an old logging road, and ends at a viewpoint and demonstration placard. Here you can look over the partially logged valley and hillsides to the coast and Gold Bluffs Beach. As the display points out, some of the scenery was logged selectively in 1945-46, while other parts were clear cut in 1965 and 1970. The landscape itself is quite instructive as to how logging operations affect the forest, and how long it takes for a logged forest to return.

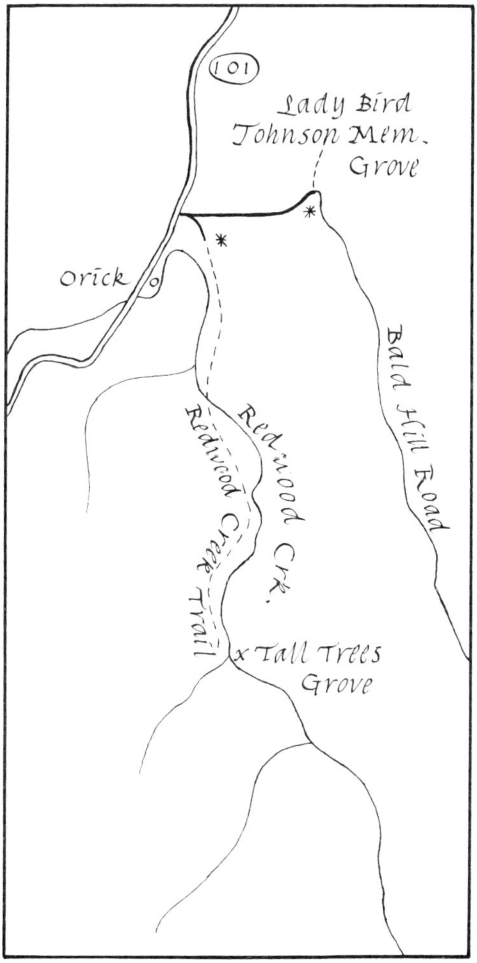

Along the trail

10 DAVISON ROAD—FERN CANYON LOOP

Prairie Creek Redwoods State Park

Drive: 26-mile loop from Orick

Road: Partly paved; partly gravel and dirt in poor condition

Hikes: Fern Canyon Loop Trail, James Irvine Trail

Features: Picnicking, camping, extended beach access, creek access, redwoods

A drive right along the coast, two hikes through the redwoods and some history are what this trip offers. To begin this loop, drive 6 miles north of Orick on U.S. 101 and turn left onto Davison Road, at a sign for Fern Canyon. This drive leads past a cow pasture, a local dairy and an inactive mill before reaching a partially paved road. The ranger at Prairie Creek Headquarters recommends using headlights on this narrow road, and exercising particular caution on the tight curves.

The initial part of the drive is through the remains of old, logged-off redwoods, where stumps and many charred trees give a ghostly testament to a forest fire. However, you soon enter second growth timber and notice many typical qualities of this general area. Ferns cover the forest floor and, in spring and early summer, skunk cabbage raise their bright yellow stalks in the marshy areas. Soon, the dense forest gives way to glimpses of the ocean.

Along part of this loop drive there is immediate access to, and views of, Gold Bluffs Beach. The name of this beach is a small reminder of the freak "gold rush" of 1851, when thousands of people were bamboozled by stories of fabulous wealth discovered in the sands and bluffs of this beach. In what must have been a frustrating experience, they attempted to separate gold from the sands, but shortly gave up. The road to the beach, however, is somewhat more rewarding.

A viewpoint above Gold Bluffs Beach can be reached by turning right at a fork in the beach road. A turn left will lead along the beach, past campgrounds and, if you are there in early spring, a small herd of Roosevelt Elk. Prairie Creek Redwoods State Park has been a game refuge

Roosevelt elk

since it was established in 1923. Presently, about 200 elk take refuge in the park. It is an exciting adventure to see these graceful, wild animals in a natural and safe, if somewhat cramped, environment. Because the elk are wild, they are safe to observe only from a distance, or from the car.

Fern Canyon Loop Trail

After Squashan Creek, pass through a grassy meadow and a grove of red alder. To the right is the six-tenths mile Fern Canyon Loop Trail (access to the canyon may also be gained by walking the James Irvine Trail). Fern Canyon was formed in the bluffs by the erosive action of Home Creek.

Beyond Fern Canyon, the drive continues past the ocean and then goes left along Ossagon Road, which returns you to U.S. 101. This section of the loop may be impassible, due to the northern road being closed in rainy seasons. Talk to the park ranger before attempting the full loop drive. When you do check at park headquarters, be sure to look for a large herd of elk grazing in the pasture next to park headquarters.

James Irvine Trail

While the main function of the James Irvine Trail is its link between park headquarters and Fern Canyon at Gold Bluffs Beach 4½ miles down the trail, the trail may also be enjoyed for its redwoods, creeks and generally rich vegetation typical of this area. The trail is named for a man who contributed to early stages in the development of the park.

From park headquarters, follow the sign to the Nature Trail. Enroute to the trailhead cross Godwood Creek, and then follow it for more than half the hike. The creek is named for John Godwood, who once homesteaded in the area.

Early in the hike, notice several marshy areas dotted with skunk cabbage and filled with patches of swamp grass. The redwoods are also plentiful, although their shallow root system leaves them vulnerable. On this hike several of the old trees have toppled.

In the first mile or so you'll frequently cross the same creek. On these various crossings, notice the bridges. All are unique, but one in particular is "paved" with redwood puncheons, with a fallen tree as crossbeam support. These bridges support ferns and moss, as well as foot traffic.

The entire round trip of 9 miles may be too much for some families. If no one can drive around to pick up the hikers where the trail ends at Davison Road, perhaps a shorter stroll along the trail, and back out the same way, would be more enjoyable.

Lupine

Redwood stump

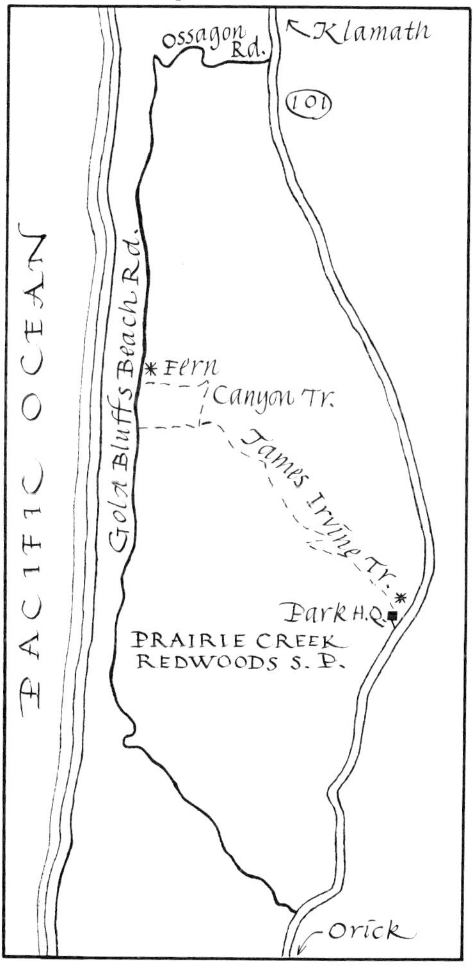

11 COASTAL DRIVE—COASTAL TRAIL

Redwood National Park

Drive: 14 miles from Requa

Road: Partly paved; partly gravel in fair condition

Hike: Coastal Trail

Features: Picnicking, beach access

The coastal drive presents an opportunity to see the weathered, northern California coast in redwood country, and the Coastal Trail provides a chance to walk a comfortable trail while in constant view of the Pacific. The drive and the hike are both memorable for scenery and history.

The Coastal Drive begins in the south, at the Alder Conservation Camp exit, or farther north, at U.S. Highway 101 and Klamath Beach Road. To take the drive from the north, turn right and follow the National Park signs, after you pass the town of Klamath and cross the Klamath River.

The narrow road which departs from U.S. 101 skirts the edge of the widening Klamath River. You will pass the remnant of a bridge that once spanned the river. In December, 1964, a flood destroyed the Douglas Memorial Bridge and the town of Klamath. The Redwood Highway and the town have been relocated but this portion of the old bridge, with its two golden bears, still stands. If you walk out to the end of this flood monument, you may see one or two little blue herons standing in the water near shore, or see other birds diving to feed.

The designated drive continues by taking the Alder Conservation Camp Road across from the old bridge. This portion of paved road connects with the Klamath Beach Road and the rest of the drive above the ocean. However, if you're feeling a little more adventurous (and if you are *not* hauling a trailer), you may continue straight on past the flood monument.

The road is narrow and winding but shaded by a luxuriant foliage of fern, maple, alder and fir. You emerge from the trees into an open area which allows you

Requa House

to see, at river level, the Klamath as it enters the ocean. The settlement of Requa is across the river. From this point on, you will be driving on dirt and gravel surfaces, so low speeds are advised. Besides, it takes time to view the ocean or, better yet, to get out of your car and explore. At a picturesque but deserted farm along the way, the vandalized buildings have partly filled with mud from the hill behind. It is a perfect spot to look at the ocean while contemplating the difficulties that this farm family must have experienced.

As you continue south you will pass the junction with Alder Camp Road before you see a huge formation of graywacke sandstone, named Split Rock. Indian legend has it that a man named Beaver anchored his fishing net to this rock with a stake. He was eager to win a fishing contest and, by help from the west wind, filled his net with so great a catch that the rock split where the anchor stake had been driven in. It may also be, as geologists tell it, that the rock broke along a joint, when strain was placed on the joint due to the erosion of lower portions of the rock.

The remainder of this 8-mile drive continues above the ocean before it angles back to U.S. 101.

Coastal Trail

The southern trailhead of the 4-mile Coastal Trail is at the end of Requa Road. If you approach the trail from this end, you have the option of visiting the Requa House, a Hurok Indian family dwelling, believed to be the oldest Indian structure in California. Although it collapsed in the 1930's, and some of the pieces and artifacts have been stolen, the house has been restored by the Del Norte County Historical Society. While it is now somewhat smaller than when first built, some of the original boards, shaped by elk horn implements, were used in the rebuilt structure. Those wishing to look around or inside the house should first get permission from Geneva Mattz, who resides in the white house across the road. Mrs. Mattz's grandmother was raised in the Requa House, and now Mrs. Mattz and her husband plan to build several more Indian structures in the vicinity, and to charge admission. When we went, however, there was no charge, and the route to the Requa House was not marked. To find the house, take Requa Road toward the southern trailhead. Pass Requa Inn and begin climbing the hill. The road is the first on the left which is not a driveway, and from the turnoff it is just a few hundred yards to the house, which stands on the hillside to your right, overlooking the mouth of the Klamath River.

The southern trailhead is farther along the paved Requa Road. This trailhead is several hundred feet up, on a seacliff above the mouth of the Klamath. The northern trailhead is at sea level, located at Lagoon Creek County Park near U.S. 101. The easiest way to take the trail is from south to north.

Views from both trailheads are powerful and exciting. Only slightly less dramatic views are possible along nearly all of the trail as it passes several inlets of rock and cliff. Exhibit plaques at viewpoints along the trail describe the occurrence of natural features. The trail passes below the 777th Air Force Base and moves sometimes along the cliff, sometimes through redwoods, fir and undergrowth.

While walking through some of the less open areas back from the edge of the cliff, the fortunate hiker will hear the barking, howling conversations of a group of sea lions. Eventually, you will be able to see them on the rocks far below, isolated by white water. A pair of binoculars makes it easier to observe the birds, sea lions, and the grey whales which migrate past each spring and early winter. The plant life along the Coastal Trail is characteristic of that along most of the northern redwoods. It includes, in addition to coastal redwood and Douglas fir: cascara, tanoak, salal, salmonberry, huckleberry, coltsfoot, lupine, bleeding heart, spring beauty, wood sorrel, stinging nettles and several others.

Coast view from U.S. 101

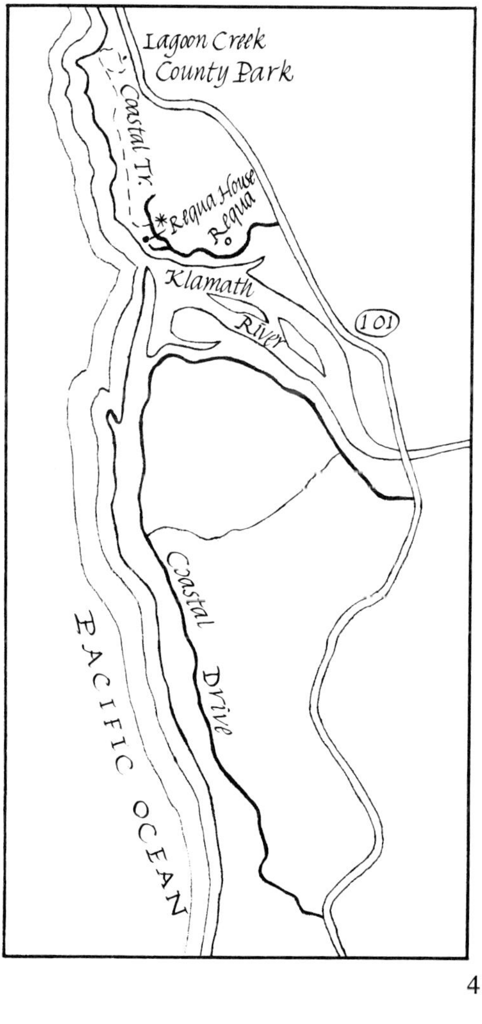

12 OLD HIGHWAY ONE

Del Norte Coast Redwoods State Park

Drive: 10 miles from Crescent City

Road: Paved

Hikes: Damnation Creek Trail—Old Hwy. 1, Nickle Creek Trail

Features: Picnicking, camping, beach access, redwoods

Portions of Highway 1 are still in use, such as that winding road leading north from the Golden Gate, but other lengths of this old highway have already been abandoned, and are now crumbling back into the redwood forest. This trip takes you along such a piece of history, and then along another section of the old roadbed which includes the shore of the Pacific.

Damnation Creek Trail—Old Hwy. 1

The trailhead for Damnation Creek Trail is 4 miles south of the Mill Creek Campground on U.S. 101. Look for a small sign, back from the highway to the west. Damnation Creek Trail is 2½ miles long, and involves a 1,000-foot drop to the ocean. The walk described here does not follow the entire trail. On the loop walk with old Route 1, you need descend along the trail only part way down the hillside of redwoods, to the blacktop of Highway 1. Remains of this old highway contour along the bluff for several miles north, along what is now the Last Chance Trail, past Enderts Beach toward Crescent City. This trip goes south, however, and is but an interesting mile along abandoned Route 1 back to 101.

As you walk along the crumbling pavement, occasionally dotted with wood sorrel, notice the reminders of the highway's past: wooden mileage posts, and an historical marker dating from 1925. The sheer drop from the highway to the ocean provides some rocky coastal scenery viewed through the thick undergrowth.

Near the end of this 1 mile on the old highway, walk up a slight hill to U.S. 101. You emerge at a sign which reads, "Divided Road 2 Miles Ahead." Walk north several hundred yards back to the Damnation Creek Trailhead and your car. Beware of trucks as they roar past you on U.S. 101. The heavy truck traffic pollutes the first and last few hundred yards of this loop walk with immense and obnoxious sounds, but the walk through the redwoods and along old Route 1 offsets this infringement.

Enderts Beach Road—Nickle Creek Trail

The Enderts Beach Road, both signed and paved, can be found on 101 south of Crescent City. The road parallels the ocean, with views of the Pacific and north to Crescent City. The road gives easy access to Crescent Beach, which is equipped with restrooms and picnic tables.

Enderts Beach Road then climbs a bluff beyond Crescent Beach to Crescent Beach Overlook, where there are more picnic tables. Just beyond the overlook is a parking area where a sign indicates: "Nickle Creek Trail, Campground 0.5, Enderts Beach 0.6, No Motor Bikes."

The Nickle Creek Trail is a wide path which looks as if it may once have been a part of the old Route 1 roadbed. The trail contours the sea cliff, then drops along a set of stairs to the picnic area, campground and beach. This easy, short drive and pleasant walk offer excellent scenery, unusual beach access, and a refreshing departure from U.S. 101.

Marker, old Route 1

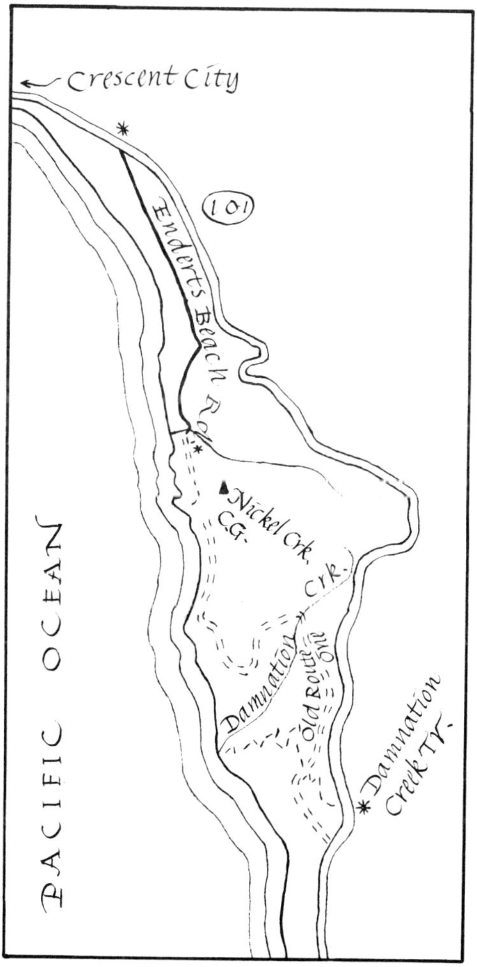

Old Route 1

13 HOWLAND HILL ROAD ROUTE 199 LOOP

Jedediah Smith Redwoods State Park

Drive: 40-mile loop from Crescent City

Road: Partly paved; partly gravel in good condition

Hikes: McKernon Trail, Boy Scout Tree Trail

Features: Picnicking, redwoods.

It is curious that Crescent City should be the beginning and end of this loop drive, because when the town was established in 1854, it could be approached only by boat. The loop of roads described here will take you through the protected old growth forest of the Jedediah Smith Redwoods State Park, named for an explorer who guided west several parties of white trappers before his death at the hands of Comanche in 1831. The Smith River, prominent in the park, also honors this man.

The loop begins just south of Crescent City, where Elk Valley Road departs from U.S. 101. A mile or two farther on Elk Valley Road, take Howland Hill Road to the right. In the early 1900's, Howland Hill Road was called the Redwood Highway, and was the main road between Crescent City and Grants Pass, Oregon. The auto traffic became so heavy that it was necessary to pave the road with redwood puncheons, or slabs, in order to support the heavier use. Today, Howland Hill Road is gravel, and this loop drive takes it only as far as U.S. 199.

Most of the trails along the loop parallel the roads, but those mentioned here lead away from the road into the redwoods. About a mile into the tall forest, watch for McKernon Trail, located on the right, before the Boy Scout Tree Trail. The latter is encountered after Howland Hill Road climbs into the forest, revealing enroute a 180 degree view of the Pacific. Both trails are unobtrusively marked, so watch for signs.

A few miles beyond the Boy Scout Tree Trailhead, Howland Hill Road crosses Mill Creek, and then follows it through the dense redwood forest. The road is narrow, and is necessarily traveled slowly. This is actually a convenience, since going slowly allows you better glimpses of the Mill Creek Valley and Mill Creek through the immense forest. There are several opportunities for picnicking or wandering afoot at turnouts, and a short side trip to Stout Memorial Grove. The Stout Grove Trail follows the Smith River a short distance, while the road also follows this river and becomes paved. Should you continue along the loop drive, you will pass through a small residential area and across a *new* covered bridge. The road soon crosses both forks of the Smith River. Turn left onto U.S. 199 towards Crescent City, passing in and out of the park, following the east side of the Smith River Valley back to town.

New covered bridge on Howland Hill Road

McKernon Trail

Be alert for this trailhead, about 1 mile into the state park. It is signed as an *unmaintained trail,* not named, and is located in front of a footbridge. The walk along the trail is mostly level, with a few obstacles such as fallen trees and branches. The only change in the easy grade occurs at the end of the three-quarters of a mile trail, as you drop to Mill Creek. The trail intersects with the Mill Creek Trail and continues along the creek to the left. McKernon Trail used to continue across Mill Creek, but unfortunately there is no bridge there now. This short walk takes you through dense forest growth. Sword fern is abundant, and the fallen logs and trees have a thick covering of moss.

Boy Scout Tree Trail

This 3-mile hike (one way) involves varied terrain. Several lengthy, steep climbs make this trail one of the more difficult in this section. The trail offers an example of the lush vegetation typical of this rainy coastal area.

The trail leads through ancient redwoods which seem unquestionably permanent in contrast to the delicate hanging moss which shrouds many of the tree limbs. The ground is thickly covered with sword and lady fern, and wood sorrel. Enjoy the abundance of such delicate wildflowers as wood violet, thimbleberry and trillium. You will also find huckleberry bushes and clumps of rhododendron. As sunlight filters through the moss and tree limbs onto patches of such undergrowth, you sense an eerie quality to the place.

Cross a small creek several times before reaching the Boy Scout Tree. This gigantic redwood has several trunks which extend from one base. You can hike 1 mile farther to Fern Falls, although many may find the round trip to the tree to be of sufficient distance.

Trillium

The Redwood Canopy

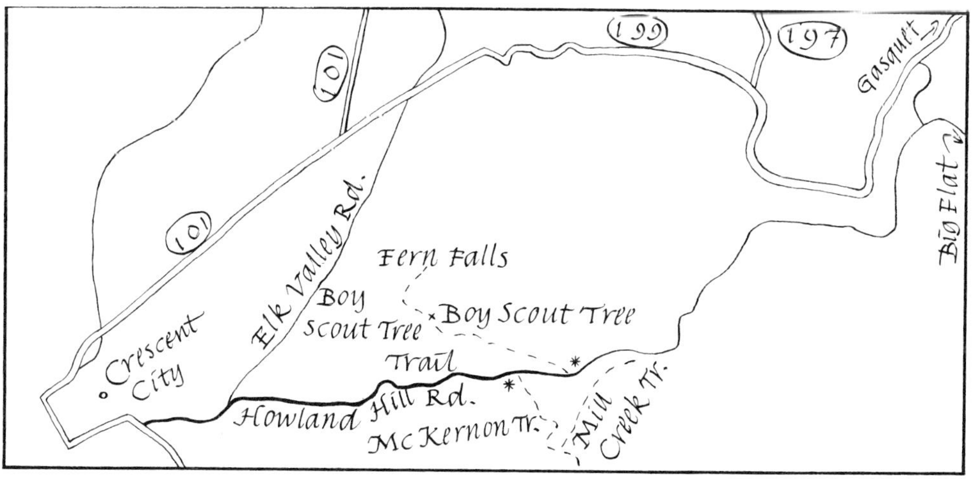

14 SMITH RIVER

Six Rivers National Forest

Drive: 40-mile loop from Crescent City

Road: Some paved; some gravel, in fair to poor condition

Hike: Upper Smith River Trail

Features: Picnicking, camping, creek and lake access

The Smith River is a mountain stream of varying appearances. At times the water rushes through ragged rock below towering canyon walls covered with Douglas fir. Then again the water may be slowly rippling over shallow expanses of the river bed. The changes are frequent and the water is always a clear blue or green. While the drive provides changing scenery, the Upper Smith River Trail allows a way to get right down to the water.

Take U.S. 199 out of Crescent City and drive approximately 12 miles to the bridge over Myrtle Creek. Cross the bridge and turn left onto the South Fork Road. It is 12 miles to Big Flat Station. Just before Big Flat take a paved road to the right, USFS 15N01, which crosses over the South Fork of the Smith. Continue climbing on road 15N01 for 2 miles and then take USFS 15N39 to the left. The road changes to gravel here. Follow it for 2 miles down through a small burn until you arrive at a flat area.

Upper Smith River Trail

Park on the flat, and walk one-fourth mile to the trailhead. This downgrade is somewhat steep but don't let it discourage you, because the trail itself is fairly level.

The trail follows along a rocky ledge above Smith River and provides the hiker with some dizzying views of the water below. While following the twisting and turning of the rock ledge, notice that the sound of the rushing river is muffled and then suddenly audible. This is caused by the rock walls which at times jut out into the trail.

After a one-fourth mile walk, cross Yellow Jacket Creek. A small waterfall tumbles into a clear water hole and provides a refreshing drink of water. Continue along the trail on an upgrade which changes to a downgrade before Buck Creek Camp. Buck Creek is a large creek which flows into Smith River. At the campground is a wooden shelter. While we recommend going this far, the trail may be followed an additional 5 miles to Gunbarrel Camp and beyond.

The Upper Smith River Trail is the western length of the old Kelsey Trail (see Trip 17) which was built in the 1860's to move supplies from Crescent City, up through the mountains, to the gold camps along Scott River.

From the trailhead, you may want to return to U.S. 199 the way you came, or you may want to continue on the loop drive. To take the loop, return on road 15N01 and intersect with South Fork Road. Turn right and head toward Big Flat Campground, which is to the left, and continue past the campground.

The remainder of the drive crosses Hurdy Gurdy Creek in several places, where you can get to the water for a picnic. Farther on pass Dry Lake, which does not live up to its name. It is a small, spring-fed lake, stocked with trout, which encourages fishermen to try their luck. We asked one oldtimer the classic question, "Having any luck?" and received the classic answer, "Yeah, all bad!"

Nearing the end of the drive you will find yourself on top of Gordon Mountain (4,143 feet). Continue 2 miles to Camp-6 Lookout and a view to the west that includes the ocean south of Crescent City, as well as the Coon Mountain Range. From the lookout to French Flat the road is steep, difficult and full of potholes, but it is passable if your car is not too low-slung From French Flat it is about 5 miles to U.S. 199.

Yellow Jacket Creek

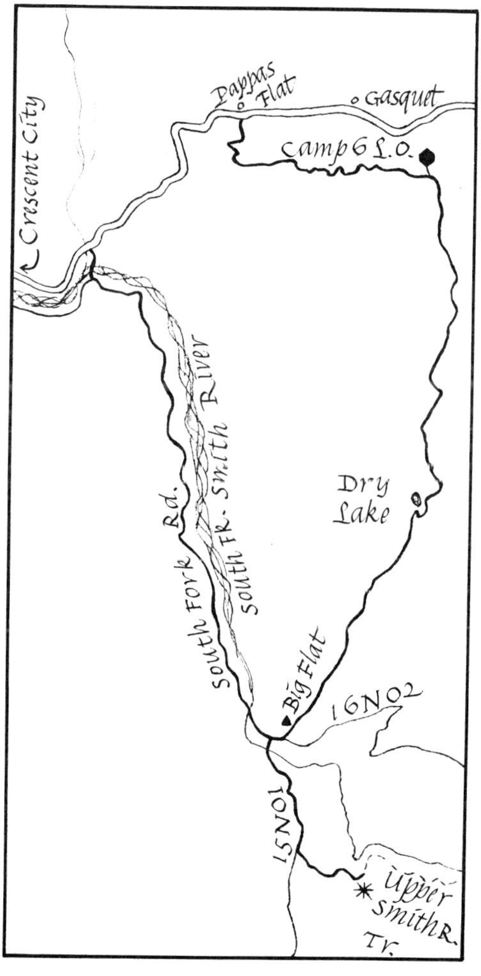

Along Smith River Loop Drive

15 NORTH BANK ROAD—LONG RIDGE LOOP

Siskiyou National Forest

Drive: 65-mile loop from Brookings

Road: Some paved; mostly gravel, in fair condition

Hikes: Upper Chetco Trail, Vulcan Lake Trail

Features: Picnicking, camping, river and lake access, wilderness area

Your family will remember this part of the southern Oregon coast and Siskiyous for its clear streams and lakes, and its unique botany. The Kalmiopsis Wilderness Area supports a number of rare plants, and the unpolluted Chetco River is considered the northern boundary for the coastal redwood. This long loop begins in Brookings, Oregon, on U.S. 101, one-quarter mile south of the Chetco Ranger Station. Wilderness area permit regulations may vary from year to year at this national forest, so stop in at the station first to see whether a permit is required. Then drive down to North Bank Road and take it inland past the Chetco River Scaling Station. The road parallels the Chetco River, which is the water supply for Brookings. The wide and brilliantly clear river seems to reflect the green hues of the surrounding fir forest. Pass Leob State Park, and then, as the pavement ends, enter federal lands.

Farther up this road (USFS 376) the national forest ends and resumes, but continue along the same road beyond the junction with USFS 3840. The latter comes down from the right, and is the other end of the loop. Continue along USFS 376 while climbing Long Ridge, and then take USFS 3917 toward Quail Prairie Lookout and Mountain. After passing Long Ridge Campground, drive through an area where the hillside is a park of fir and braken fern. The Douglas fir are especially fertilized and pruned for the production of fir cones, which are collected to provide seeds for reforestation.

Quail Prairie Lookout (3,033 feet) is signed, and is up a short road to the left. The view from there includes several clear cut areas, and on each logged hillside are long, spoke-like gouges caused by dragging the logs uphill from where they were felled. It is interesting, in any logged area, to try to guess when the area was cut judging by the degree of erosion on these gouged hillsides.

Wild azalea

Upper Chetco Trail

Shortly beyond the lookout is the Upper Chetco Trail. The trail goes for many miles, at first skirting the western boundary and then crossing the Kalmiopsis Wilderness Area in what must be a splendid week-long hike. You can walk for just a mile or so, through fir, rhododendron, bear grass, pine and braken, to get views of Johnson Butte to the east and south.

The rugged samples of the Siskiyous given by the lookout and the Upper Chetco Trail can be improved upon by continuing the drive, as the road narrows, and then by taking the side road and trail to Vulcan Lake.

Turn right a little over 3 miles beyond the lookout and trail, following signs to Vulcan Lake and Vulcan Peak. This side road drops to cross Boulder Creek at a switchback, and then climbs to the wilderness boundary. This 6-mile road is in fairly good condition, except for the last mile, which is very rough and must be driven slowly. The road ends where a pit and wall have been built at the wilderness boundary to exclude motorized vehicles.

Vulcan Lake Trail

The 1-mile trail seems longer than that, because the first two-thirds mile climbs a ridge, and the remainder drops down to spring-fed Vulcan Lake, which drains into a smaller lake nearby. If the magnificent scenery from the top does not make the trip worthwhile, then a plunge into the cool, clear lake will. Be alert for Kalmiopsis, the prehistoric member of the Heath family for which the wilderness area is named. Do not destroy the plants, as things grow very slowly here, and it could take years to recover from the mishap of a single step or act of vandalism. Near the lake, a trail forks uphill to Vulcan Peak. The lower trail leads to the lake.

From the turnoff to the Vulcan Lake Trail, USFS 3840D leads down to USFS 3840, which crosses and then follows Quail Prairie Creek, and reconnects with USFS 376. The Chetco River along this stretch of road is a popular swimming area, and you can stop for a dip if you missed out at Vulcan Lake or along Quail Prairie Creek.

The Kalmiopsis Wilderness Area is complexly unique. A part of the Siskiyou Mountains, it is older (Mesozoic or older) than either the adjoining Coastal or Cascade Ranges, and thus has produced a differing geology and soil composition. Because of this, and its altitude and location, plants are found here which ordinarily are found only many miles away. In the case of some pre-ice age plants such as *Kalmiopsis leachiana,* these old mountains support botany which otherwise would long have been extinct. For access into the Kalmiopsis Wilderness Area from the east, please consult Trip 25. The rare Kalmiopsis plants can be found in several large patches which bloom, elusively, in June or July. If you are lucky enough to see the Kalmiopsis in bloom, please enjoy it where it is. To quote the Forest Service: "Because of its extreme rarity, this plant is given complete protection. No part of the plant may be collected without a special written permit, and the issuance of these permits is restricted to scientific purposes only." Those interested in hiking to one of these large areas can contact the Chetco Ranger Station for directions.

Vulcan Lake

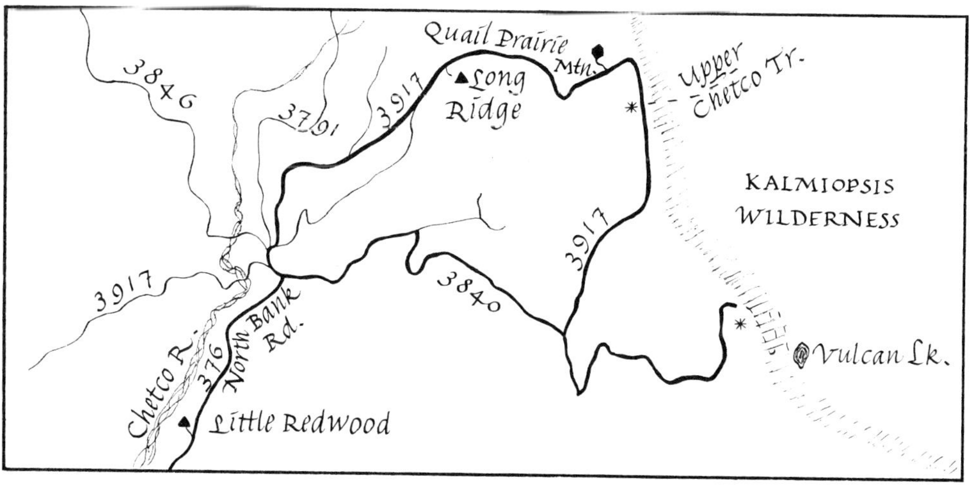

Quail Prairie Mtn.
Long Ridge
Upper Chetco Tr.
KALMIOPSIS WILDERNESS
3846
3791
3917
3917
3917
3840
North Bank Rd.
376
Chetco R.
Little Redwood
Vulcan Lk.

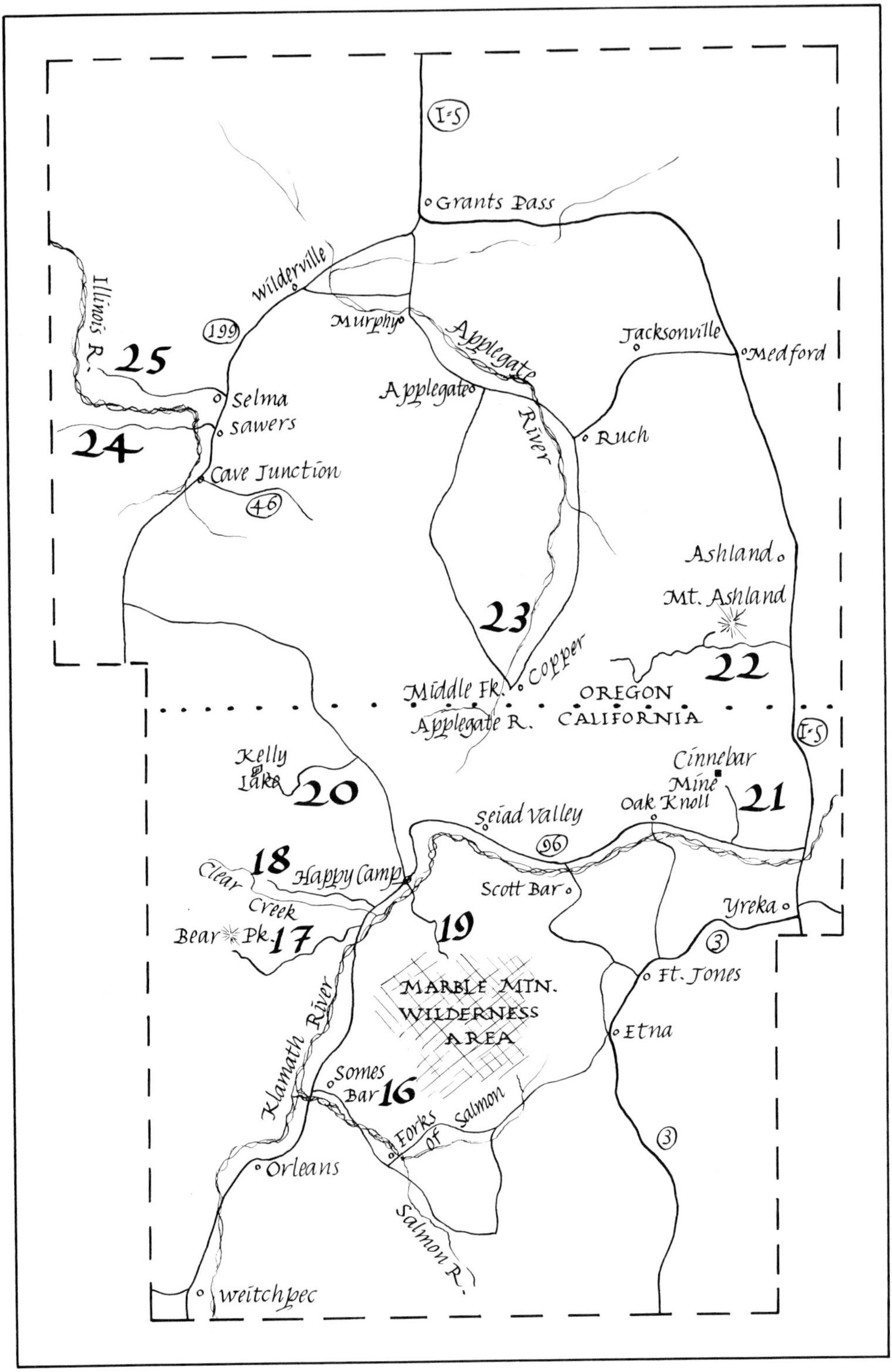

I-5
Grants Pass
Wilderville
199
Illinois R.
25
Selma
Sawers
24
Cave Junction
46
Murphy
Applegate
Applegate River
Jacksonville
Medford
Ruch
Ashland
Mt. Ashland
23
22
Copper
Middle Fk.
Applegate R.
OREGON
CALIFORNIA
I-5
Kelly Lake
20
Cinnebar Mine
21
Oak Knoll
Seiad Valley
96
18
Happy Camp
Clear Creek
Scott Bar
Yreka
Bear Pk.
17
19
3
Ft. Jones
MARBLE MTN. WILDERNESS AREA
Etna
Klamath River
Somes Bar
16
Forks of Salmon
Orleans
3
Salmon R.
Weitchpec

III. Klamath River & The Siskiyous

As you follow the Klamath River and California 96 west from Interstate 5, watch the rocks along the river for blue heron. These blue, long-beaked and long-legged birds sit and feed along the river, often looking as much like driftwood as birds. Along with the unusual wildlife, you will also find evidence of local history. The Klamath runs through mining country, and along much of its course are tailings —tall, long piles of rock put there last century mainly by the Chinese who were brought in to search and mine for gold. Man has more recently contributed another characteristic to the river, seen as large chunks of white foam floating along the surface, over the rapids, past the blue heron, to be trapped into swirling eddies along the bank. What is this material and where does it come from? If it bothers you, ask around—it's something the locals are concerned about.

The Klamath River runs west between the Siskiyous and the Scott Bar Mountains. Between Seiad Valley and Happy Camp it turns and begins meandering on a southerly course. It is south of Happy Camp that the Off Fire (Trip 16) occurred, and it is here that the first trip of this section leads. By examining the mountainous edges of the fire, you can see how it climbed and spread, and how the forest recovers, with a little help from the Forest Service.

The mountains south of Happy Camp all but demand exploring, and the next three trips take you there. The Bear Peak Trail along Kelsey Range (Trip 17) is one of ridgetop scenery and history, while the drive and hike along Clear Creek (Trip 18) show a remarkably clear and blue mountain stream. The three trails in the Elk Creek drainage system (Trip 19) lead to more streams and their small valleys.

Indian Creek Road (Trip 20) goes north of Happy Camp to a small mountain lake, one of the few in the Klamath Mountains that is easily accessible.

The mountains east of Happy Camp, back along California 96, are less remarkable for their scenery, but can still be appreciated for their character and for the minerals they once bore. The trip to Cinnebar Mine up Empire Creek Road (Trip 21) shows something of both.

The Siskiyou Mountains seem smooth, high and dry as they drop to the Klamath, but on their northern slopes they are forested and rugged. The trip up to Mt. Ashland (Trip 22) and along the Siskiyou Divide reveals the summits of this range. Trip 23, to the Middle Fork of the Applegate River, leads into one of the most prominent valleys and most beautiful areas of the Siskiyous. The next trip, up Eight Dollar Mountain Road to Onion Camp (Trip 24), begins in Grants Pass, Oregon, crosses the Applegate, and then leads back up into the Siskiyous. At the end of the road are two large wild onion patches and two trails: one to a mountain lake, and the other to the Kalmiopsis Wilderness Area Boundary. Also beginning in Grants Pass, the final trip in both this section and the book is along the Illinois River (Trip 25). Some of the drive, and both trails, feature the rocks, forests and drama of this green, wild river.

This entire section is mountainous enough to make travel impossible, or at best dangerous, while there is snow on the ground. In summer, the nights are cool, but the temperature often rises to over 100 degrees in the daytime.

16 THE OFF FIRE

Klamath National Forest

Drive: 61 miles from Happy Camp

Road: Some paved; mostly gravel in poor to good condition

Hikes: Hike behind Camp Three, Wooley Creek Trail

Features: Picnicking, camping

While touring a recent forest fire is not the usual vacation fare, a trip through the Off Fire is included because nothing educates so well as the "real thing." The area will serve, for years, as an example of how a forest returns from the devastation of fire.

The burn is 35 miles south of Happy Camp, close to the junction of California Highway 96 and Forest Highway 93. The Off Fire started July 27, 1973, and because it started near Highway 96, away from any campgrounds, it is thought that the fire could not have been started by campers. It *is* believed to have been man-caused, however, and possibly to have been deliberately set.

Man caused 9,200 acres of timber to be destroyed. The sawtimber loss was approximately 10,000,000 board feet, although the Forest Service hopes to salvage-log half of that. The real loss was that much of the burn was in plantation, or pole timber, too young for the mill. The fire destroyed five residences and damaged two others. No human life was lost, but the toll of death and disruption to wildlife is inestimable.

The fire, which takes its name from nearby Offield Mountain, required 2,000 people, including support personnel, to control it. The blaze was declared controlled after nearly seven days of fighting.

To get to the Off Fire, drive 35 miles south on California 96 from Happy Camp. Turn left off 96 onto Offield Mountain Lookout Road (USFS 15N17), about 1½ miles before the junction of State Highway 96 and Forest Highway 93. The first part of the drive is paved but rough. Because

Off Fire Trail

of high winds at the time the fire jumped from place to place. Frequently trees were killed from heat and left uncharred, and thus they retained their limbs and dry, dead foliage. All underbrush and ground cover was consumed, leaving dried or ash-covered earth. In a few miles a sign on the right denotes: "Sulphur Springs." (This is a rough road which deadends at a creek, providing a pleasant picnic spot.)

Continue on 15N17, until a sign at a fork in the road, "Offield Lookout, 2 miles," indicates a sharp turn to the left. At the lookout (4,116 feet) there is a broad view of the Klamath River flowing north to south. Also, frequent dry patches of dead trees can be seen juxtaposed with green fir.

A few hundred yards from the lookout sign on 15N17, turn right onto USFS 12N52. This road goes down through a burned area, providing a graphic example of how the fire jumped and traveled. From this junction, it is 4 miles to Camp Three.

Hike Behind Camp Three

At the farthest end of Camp Three, cat tracks lead from the right side of the road. Park alongside the road and, crossing the creek, enter the burn from here. You will find a hill devoid of trees, with occasional piles of charred stumps heaped together for eventual destruction. Despite the grim view, deer and bear tracks may be seen in the powdery soil. Animals, deer in particular, like to roll in the fresh ashes of a forest fire, to rid themselves of ticks. Walk as long as you like, or take in the creek several hundred feet from the road, that flows through the still green forest bordering the area.

For a different view of the fire, return on 15N17 and turn left upon reaching Highway 96. The view along this portion of highway includes several of the fire-damaged homes. The scorched trees are particularly twisted and the earth blackened. At the intersection of California 96 and Forest Highway 93 go straight ahead on 93 to a sign on the right, designating the former site of Somes Bar. Founded by the gold miner Abraham Somes in 1860, the small town once consisted of a store, post office and hotel. The last remains of this settlement were destroyed by the 1955 flood. Mr. Somes was not the only gold miner to enter the area; in fact, there was mining throughout the Salmon River Basin. During part of the Gold Rush, two hundred mules packed 3,000 tons of goods over the Salmon Mountains yearly to supply the mining camps.

Wooley Creek Trail

A little over 1 mile past Oak Bottom Campground there is a small sign on the left: "Trail 7E13, 5 miles." This trail is recommended, at least for some distance, so that you can see more of the burn and fire fighting techniques. Some of the trees along the trail have been uprooted because the fire would otherwise smoulder in their roots, causing it to burst out anew. Notice also the pits where fire fighters literally dug smouldering roots and stumps from the ground. The trail is rocky and switchbacks lead up the side of the ridge. From this point there is a view of the Salmon River below.

Desolation near Camp 3

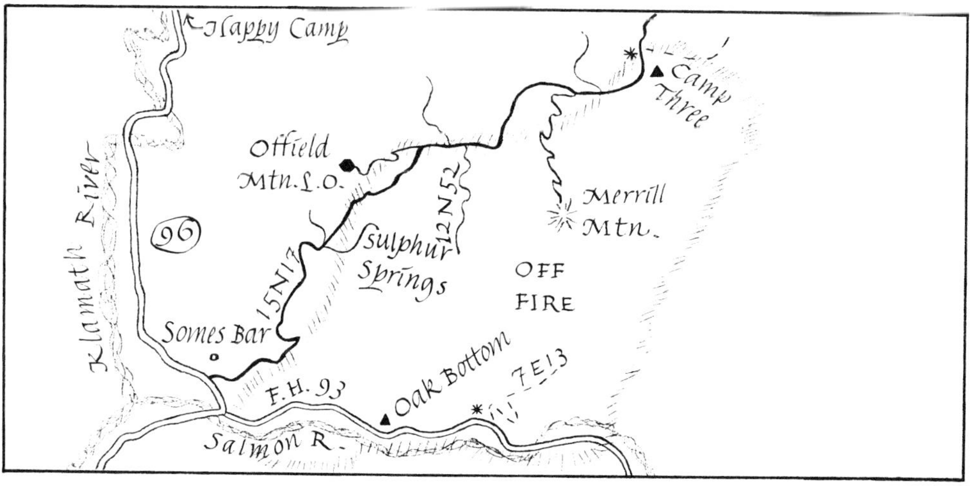

17 BEAR PEAK—KELSEY RANGE

Klamath National Forest

Drive: 22 miles from Happy Camp

Road: Gravel and dirt in fair condition

Hike: Bear Peak Trail

Features: Mountain lake access, ridgetop scenery

This area of the Siskiyou Mountains is impressive for its scenery and intriguing for its history. An historical marker has been placed just across Highway 96 from the turnoff for this drive. Here, each August until 1929, the Karok Indians held a Pikiawish, or world renewal celebration, to insure an abundance of acorns and salmon. To get to this historic site, and the turnoff to the drive, go south of Happy Camp 12 miles to Bear Peak Road.

The drive goes west along Bear Peak Road (USFS 15N19), uphill away from Highway 96 and the Klamath River, 12.6 miles (including the trail) to Bear Peak. Along the 10 miles or so to the trail, the road climbs to the top, where the view opens to ridge after ridge of mountains, as far as you can see.

Bear Peak Trail

The trail is signed: "Bear Peak Trail—Elbow Springs." Aside from some patches of snow early in the season, Elbow Springs is the only source of water between the car and Bear Lakes. The small volume of this spring and the steep descent to the lakes are such that you may want to carry a little water, especially on a warm day.

The 2½ to 3 mile trail climbs, gently but steadily, to Bear Peak, with Dillon Divide visible to the left. Near the trail are such wildflowers as alpine shooting star, wood violet and spreading phlox, as well as the evergreens kinnikinnick, Douglas fir, mountain hemlock, cedar and tanoak.

The trail leads about one-quarter of a mile down to Bear Lake, and a little farther to Lower Bear Lake and the Little Bear Valley. The trail can be located on the saddle between Bear Peak (5,740 feet) and Red Hill (5,642 feet). Unless you enjoy steep trails, consider this side trail as an option until, looking down to the north from the saddle, you can judge for yourself whether these appealing little lakes are inviting enough for you.

Looking west from this junction toward Red Hill notice that the trail dims as it extends out onto Kelsey Ridge. The trail to Bear Peak and beyond is the remnant of the Kelsey Trail, which was built in the 1860's. It was used as a pack trail to bring provisions through the mountains from Crescent City to the gold camps. It took pack mules nineteen days to make the trip, from Crescent City into the Scott River area and back. (See Trip 15 for a hike on the western length of the old Kelsey Trail.)

Bear Lake

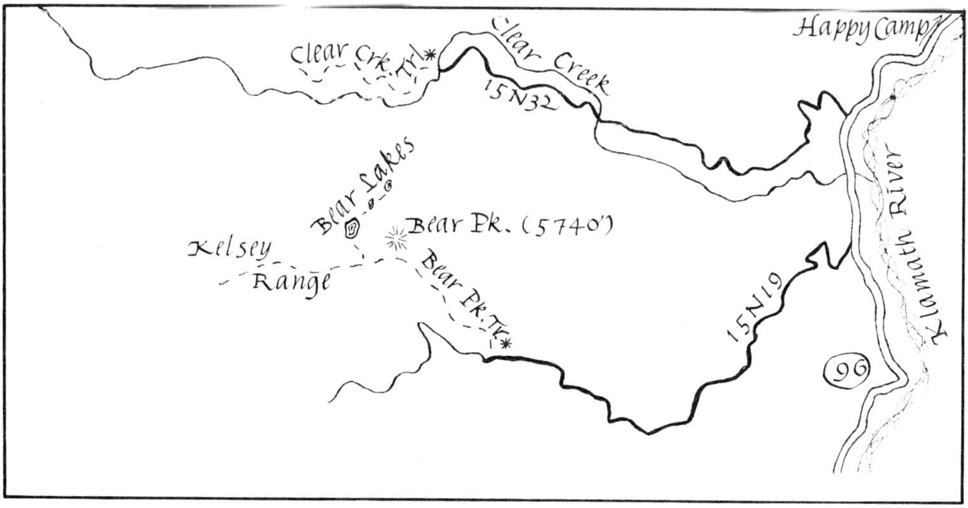
Happy Camp
Clear Crk. Trl.
Clear Creek
15N32
Bear Lakes
Bear Pk. (5740')
Kelsey
Range
Bear Pk. Tr.
15N19
Klamath River
96

18 CLEAR CREEK

Klamath National Forest

Drive: 16 miles from Happy Camp

Road: Partly paved; partly gravel, in good to poor condition

Hike: Clear Creek Trail

Features: Picnicking, primitive camping, mountain stream access

This drive is, at times, difficult, but is more than worth the effort to see a creek of such a deep and striking blue. It is the beauty of Clear Creek which makes getting to the trail worthwhile.

Drive approximately 6 miles south from Happy Camp on California 96. This portion of the Klamath River Highway was once a pack trail, used during the Gold Rush of the 1850's. The turnoff is across from Wingate Bar. A sign on the left indicates that it is 10 miles to Clear Creek Trail.

The road, which is paved to the first fork, is frequently steep, and we would discourage hauling a trailer along it. The road may be impassable in early spring, so check with the ranger in Happy Camp before embarking on it.

In the first few miles of the drive, the effects of a recent fire are visible. Called the Wingate Fire, it covered approximately 825 acres. Like the Off Fire, farther south, it is thought to be man-caused, but fortunately this fire was contained within one day by fire fighting operations. When we went through, the scorched, dead trees were still standing. Depending upon how long after the fire you are driving through, you will see either a newly salvage-logged area, or a logged burn that is being regenerated by seeding, both by the Forest Service and by the forest itself. It will, however, be many years before the burn reassumes the appearance of a forest.

At the first fork in the road keep to the left, and continue on graded gravel for several miles. Pass Fivemile Creek and later, Clear Creek, and then keep to the right. From here on the road is quite rough, and the use of first gear is advised.

Clear Creek Trail

The trailhead is at the end of a bridge over Clear Creek. Walk across to a large, cleared area which contains a rustic table. This is a primitive campsite, so you will have to make your own provisions for fuel and toilet facilities.

A sign indicates the direction of the Clear Creek Trail, which extends for about one-quarter mile to a steep hill. We could not locate the trail beyond this point, but were told by the Forest Service that it should be cleared by about the time this book is on the market. If and when the brushing has been completed, you will be able to hike farther than indicated here. Otherwise, the short walk allows another way to get down to the water, and there is also fishing and swimming near the rocks below the bridge.

Clear Creek

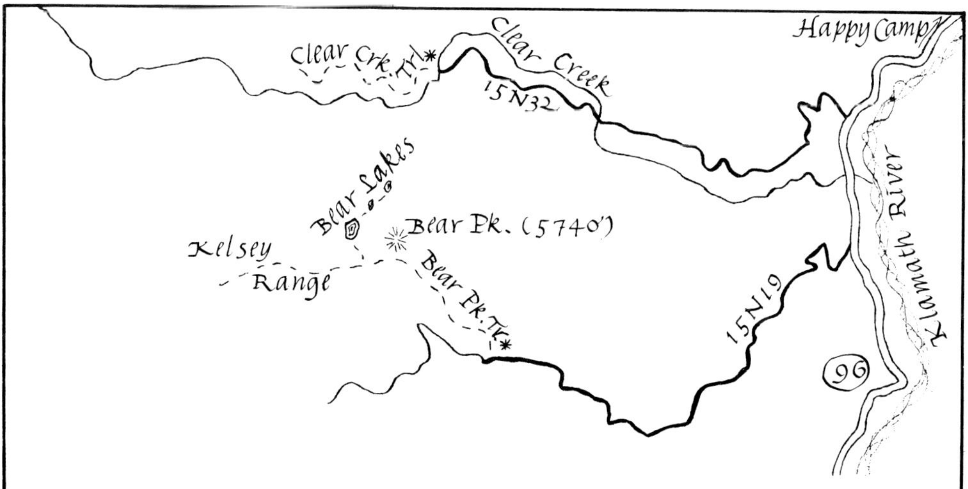

Happy Camp
Clear Creek
Clear Crk. Trl.
15N32
Bear Lakes
Bear Pk. (5740')
Kelsey Range
Bear Pk. Tr.
15N19
Klamath River
96

19 ELK CREEK DRAINAGE

Klamath National Forest

Drive: 12 miles from Happy Camp

Road: Mostly paved, but rough in spots

Hikes: Lick Creek Trail, Elk Creek Trail, Bear Creek Trail

Features: Picnicking, camping, mountain stream access, wilderness area

This paved road into the mountains leads along a valley to within 4 miles of the Marble Mountain Wilderness Area, and to three trails which go into the wilderness area. Those intending to walk into the wilderness area should first obtain a permit at the ranger station in Happy Camp.

At the south end of Happy Camp, turn from California 96 onto Elk Creek Road. Cross a bridge and then turn right, following this paved county road through the Elk Creek Watershed. Here you can enjoy views of the forest, and some rugged facets of the Klamath Mountains. The route parallels Elk Creek, and is surfaced to within 1 mile of Sulphur Springs Campground.

Lick Creek and Elk Creek Trails

In order to picnic or camp at Sulphur Springs, gear and supplies must be carried over a bridge across Elk Creek. This bridge is also crossed for access to Lick Creek and Elk Creek trails. At the far side of the bridge, the campground is to the right, the trails, to the left.

Quite soon Lick Creek Trail (8E04) leads uphill to the right, while Elk Creek Trail (8E05) leads to the left. Lick Creek Trail rises steeply, and then follows above the creek, eventually passing the headwaters of the creek and intersecting with Trail 7E02, which leads into the wilderness area. It is apparent from the start that Lick Creek Trail could be a worthwhile but strenuous hike.

Elk Creek Trail crosses Lick Creek soon after the junction, and then the view opens to include Elk Creek, which the trail follows for several miles. The forest is dense here, resulting in a cool, shady hike along a trail which is gentle, at least for the first mile or two. This trail was part of a pack trail system used in the mid-1800's, once connecting with Indian Creek Trail, the trail along the Klamath River which is now Highway 96, and the old Kelsey Trail, all of which are covered elsewhere in this book.

Bear Creek Trail

The third trail on this trip begins in a clearing at the end of the road, 2 unpaved miles beyond Sulphur Springs Campground. As you come into the clearing, the little trail to the right (southeast) leads along Elk Creek to an irrigation ditch. Another trail near there takes you down to Elk Creek, but the Bear Creek Trail is on the left (north).

The Bear Creek Trail (8E06) is a bit more demanding than the last one, but it gives you waterfalls. Through similarly dense forest, this trail climbs steeply, then gently, then steeply again, presenting views of the canyon and river below, and finally coming alongside the creek. Here, a set of falls furnish the environment for a picnic. Beyond the falls the trail climbs gently to an intersecting creek. Along this stretch are several places where you can get over to Bear Creek, or you may explore the trail for some of its several miles as it approaches and enters the wilderness area.

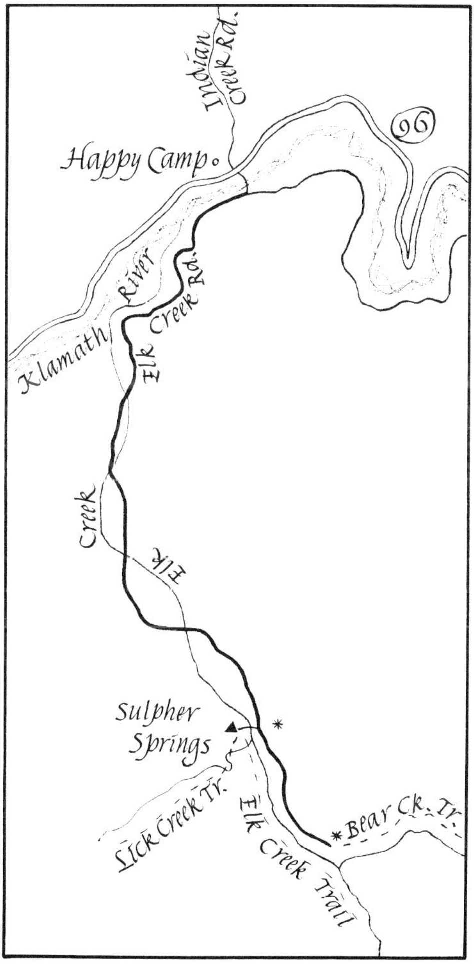

Elk Creek Trail

20 INDIAN CREEK ROAD TO KELLY LAKE

Klamath National Forest

Drive: 17 miles from Happy Camp

Road: Mostly paved; some gravel, in fair condition

Hikes: Kelly Lake Trail, Nature Trail

Features: Picnicking, camping, mountain lake access

This trip might be taken for several reasons, two of the most likely being that the drive is mostly on paved road, and that the walk to the lake is only a quarter of a mile long.

From Happy Camp, which was originally a gold camp set up in 1852, take Indian Creek Road through town and past the high school, or take Davis Road from California 96 and then pick up Indian Creek Road north of town. This good, shady, county road follows Indian Creek, and the route of an old pack trail, through the length of a narrow strip of private property, 13 miles to West Branch Campground. Although pavement ends just across Kemper Creek, the remaining 2 miles of gravel to the campground are adequate.

Just before the campground, take USFS 18N27 and climb through forest and then a desolate, logged burn, following the signs to Kelly Lake. When there is 1 mile to go, get onto USFS 18N30, climbing to a view, on the left, of Mt. Shasta.

Kelly Lake Trail and Nature Trail

The one-quarter mile walk to the lake is easy. The lake is very clear, deeper than it looks, and stocked with trout. A short nature trail leads north and west of the lake which might be of interest, providing that vandals have not, as sometimes happens, removed the signs which mark this trail.

Kelly Lake

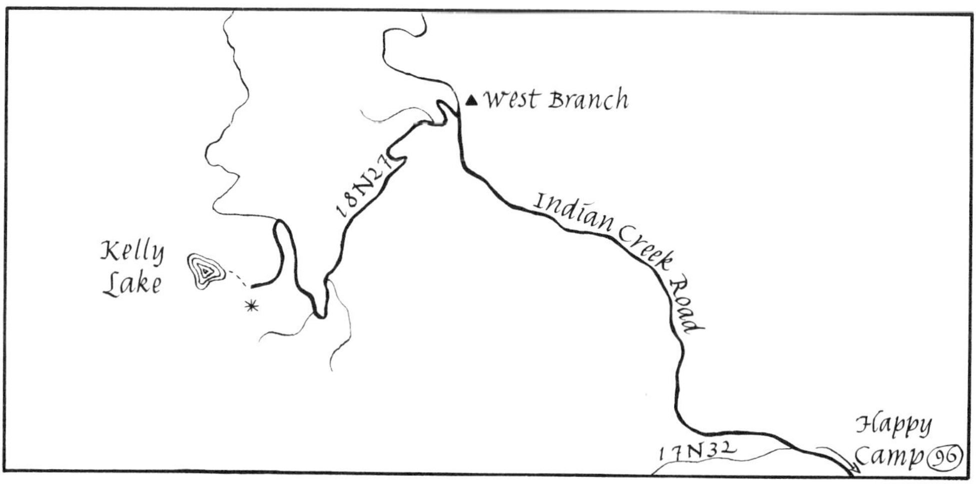
West Branch
18N27
Indian Creek Road
Kelly
Lake
Happy
Camp
96
17N32

21 CINNEBAR MINE—EMPIRE CREEK ROAD

Klamath National Forest

Drive: 13 miles from Interstate 5

Road: Dirt and gravel, in poor condition

Hike: Walk to Cinnebar Mine

Features: Picnicking, creek access, abandoned mine

On a spring day or summer morning, this drive and easy walk can offer good scenery, cool shade and an abandoned mercury mine. The drive begins where the Empire Creek Road (signed, "Empire Creek") leads north from Highway 96, about 10 miles west of I-5. Keep to the right at every junction. Drive along Empire Creek for over 3 miles.

About half-way in, pass the wooden remains of some sort of mill. On the hillside above the mill is a barbed wire fence, built along a hand-dug irrigation ditch. Just across the road, notice the stone foundation and fruit trees of a burned down house. All that is left above the steps is a flat area spiked with mullein stalks. Perhaps 1 mile beyond these ruins, pass a burned house, the aluminum siding of which can be seen from the road. Buildings such as these were once built on unpatented mine claims. When these claims are declared "null and void," the Forest Service reclaims the land. Since Forest Service regulations prohibit such buildings on their land, they allow the claim holders to remove whatever lumber and materials they want, and then the rest is burned.

Less than 1 mile beyond that last burned house is an unmarked road leading left, uphill to the mine. The Empire Creek Road once connected with the Beaver Creek Road, another dirt road which comes out at Hilt on I-5. Beyond the turnoff to the mine, however, the road is no longer maintained, and your vehicle could get stuck if you go too much farther. Similarly, the road up to the mine is better walked than driven.

Walk to Cinnebar Mine

Park at the junction and walk the rocky road as it contours, gently climbing through sagebrush and oak, about three-quarters of a mile to the Cinnebar Mine. The mine is named for the vermillion-colored mercuric oxide, called cinnebar, from which mercury is refined.

Near the mine, the upper road will lead to the collapsed shaft, which is partially filled with water. It would be possible to wade several yards into the shaft, but we advise against it. The lower road leads to concrete foundations, twisted framework, a water tank and other paraphernalia.

In summer, the walk is best taken in sturdy shoes, in the cool of the morning, leaving the hot afternoon to be spent back along the creek or the Klamath.

Cinnebar Mine shaft

Along Empire Creek Road

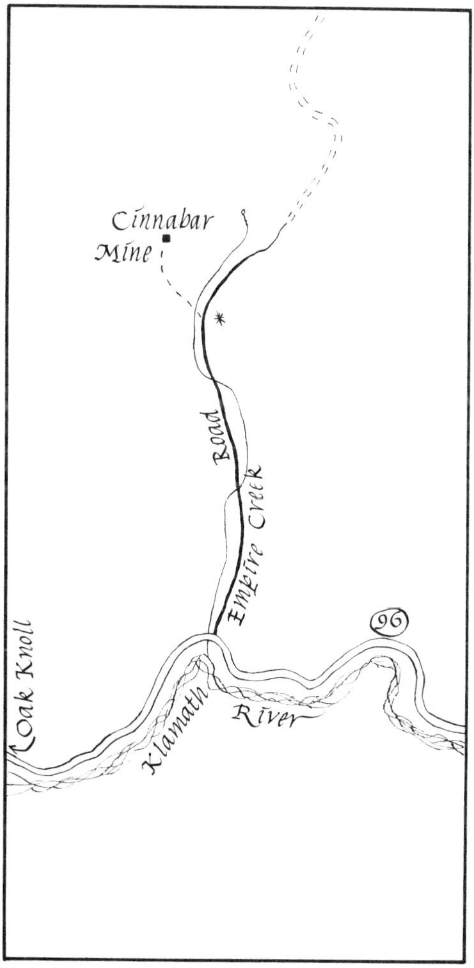

22 MT. ASHLAND—SISKIYOU DIVIDE

Klamath and Rogue River National Forests

Drive: 25 miles from Ashland

Road: Partly paved, partly gravel, in fair condition

Hike: Seven Mile Ridge Trail

Features: Picnicking, camping, mountain meadows

Should you be in Ashland, Oregon for the Shakespearean Festival, or if you are interested in high roads, pleasant walks, alpine picnics and mountain scenery, spend some time on this trip. Take the Mt. Ashland Ski Bowl exit, off Interstate 5, about 10 miles south of Ashland. Down the road a bit turn right onto Colestin Road, following signs to the Mt. Ashland Ski Area.

The pavement lasts until the ski buildings, which are closed in the summer. The only road up there (USFS 392) goes past the ski area, leading on dirt and gravel to the Mt. Ashland Picnic Area. With its view, water, fireplaces and outhouses, this is a nice spot, but there are other good picnic areas down the road.

One place of interest is the top of the mountain, gained by a signed side road not far beyond the picnic area. At the end of this rough, 1 mile side trip is the Mt. Ashland Weather Radar Site, the buildings and equipment used by the scientists, and a ski lift which is inoperative in summer. At the parking area you can climb one of the two peaks for a better view, or just walk around while enjoying what there is to see from there.

Back down on USFS 392, the main part of the drive goes along the upper road at the first intersection past the road to the summit. Take the lower road, however, for a pleasant, if unofficial, picnic area where there is water, a meadow and a view, but no facilities and hence, please, no fires or camp stoves. Road USFS 392 still leads west, crossing the Willamette Meridian and Forest Service turnout and viewpoint.

The road will lead all the way to Applegate, but we describe the way only as far as Wrangle Campground, which can be driven to along a signed side road to the right. A stone community shelter is prominent at this otherwise primitive campground. Springwater flows from the T-joint of a pipe up near the back of the meadow (if you listen, you'll hear it). The tall, spaceship-like object in the meadow is used for measuring snowfall, while nearby is a locked shelter for the use of snow crews.

Seven Mile Ridge Trail

A road drops steeply from the campground. Down this track is the Seven Mile Ridge Trail (939) which leads north, across Old Jack Creek and Old Jack Flat. As the trail contours the ridges, you will have excellent views of the Siskiyou Mountains, which are more rugged than their recent reputation might suggest. You may be distracted from the green and misty scenery by wildflowers, among them white hellebore, yarrow, groundsel and aster fleabane.

Community shelter at Wrangle Campground

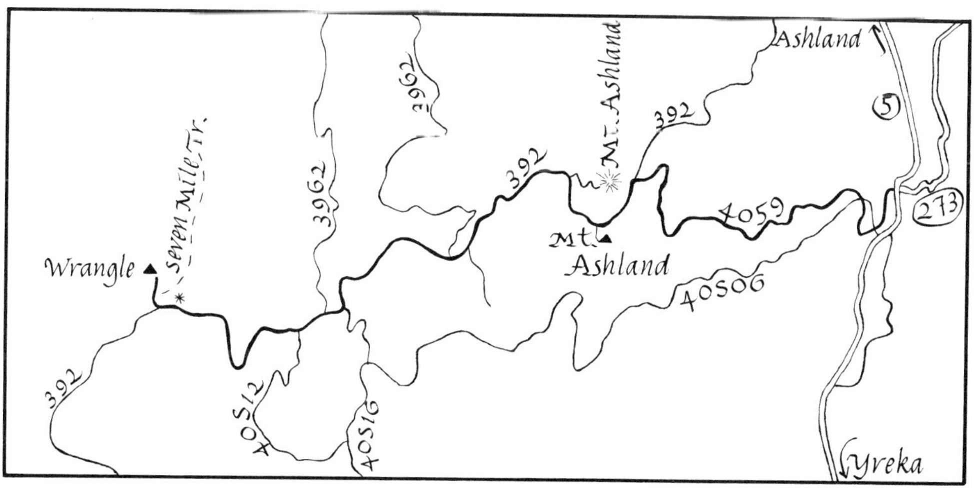

MIDDLE FORK APPLEGATE RIVER

Rogue River National Forest

Drive: 30 miles from Medford; 43 miles from Grants Pass

Road: Mostly paved; some gravel, in fair to good condition

Hike: Middle Fork Trail

Features: Picnicking, camping, mountain river access

The Upper Applegate area of northern California and southern Oregon is one of old forests, clear swift rivers and farmland, set amidst years of colorful history and the Siskiyou Mountains. This trip extends into Oregon via Jacksonville, although the same area can be reached over rougher roads from Mt. Ashland, by following the Siskiyou Summit Road (USFS 392) mentioned in Trip 22. From Medford, take Oregon 238 through Jacksonville. The trip can also be begun at Grants Pass, by taking Oregon 238 south from town. The drive from Grants Pass to Murphy follows the flat, winding Applegate River Valley past farms, and views of the Siskiyou Mountains. From the lumber and farm town of Murphy, to Provolt, the scenery includes fir and big maples. After Provolt there are more farms, and maples, oaks and Douglas firs. West of the town of Applegate you will find a suspension foot bridge across the Applegate—an interesting side trip for those who dare. A road to the right after the bridge leads to Cantrall Buckley Park. This drive along the Applegate from Grants Pass is of such pleasant beauty that it can be recommended as an extension of the drive from Medford. From either direction, turn off at Ruch, and follow the Applegate River Road to the community of Copper, named for the Blue Ledge Mine, which closed in 1929 but which some day may be reopened.

Just past Copper, turn left at the fork and follow USFS 41S01 for 7 miles, through the proposed site of the Applegate Dam and Reservoir. The dam is part of a U.S. Army Corps of Engineers project to put three dams in the Rogue River Basin. Construction has begun on the other two sites, but has been delayed at this site by lack of funds from Congress, which authorized the project in 1962. Local citizens and conservationists are opposing the project. According to the Army Corps of Engineers and the Forest Service, the dam would provide "flood control, fishery enhancement, recreation and irrigation." Those opposed to the dam assert that there are less expensive ways to deal with flooding in the sparsely populated area downstream. They point out that while some fishing may be enhanced, steelhead and salmon will be blocked from natural spawning areas, and that other wildlife will be diminished. Dam opponents assert that several local lake or reservoir recreation sites are already in use, and feel that a clear, free flowing mountain stream is therefore of greater recreational benefit. Finally, they say that irrigation benefits would be small, that no plans have yet been made to use them, and that while some now have rights to naturally flowing water, those rights do not apply to impounded water. If and when the $47 million rockfill dam is constructed, 988 acres will be flooded, creating a lake 4½ miles long. The present access road will be replaced, but the upper part of the drive and the entire trail described below should be subjected to little change.

Middle Fork Trail

About 7 miles beyond the proposed damsite, the sign to the trailhead is found in a wide spot in the road. Walk in a quarter mile to the trailhead. The trail parallels the Middle Fork of the Applegate River, and so makes river access easy and enjoyable. In fact, of the several trails in the immediate area, this is the only one with frequent and easy river access. The trail is quite level for most of the walk which, for our purposes, ends at the second log bridge.

Changes in the river are part of what makes this hike exciting. At some places, the water flows over solid rock, creating a pleasing contrast between the swift, green current and the hard, grey rock. At other points the river may rush through a small funnel of rock, causing the cascade of gushing water.

While continuing the hike, watch for a small waterfall spilling down the mountainside, opposite the trail. Just beyond the falls the trail forks to the right, while to the left a log bridge leads to the still active Lil' Hon Mine. The trail leads up above the river, contouring the mountainside, and then drops down to a bridge made out of a large, uprooted log. It is about 2 miles to this bridge, and while the trail continues on uphill, it was this 4 mile walk along the river and back that we wanted you to enjoy.

Bridge over Applegate River

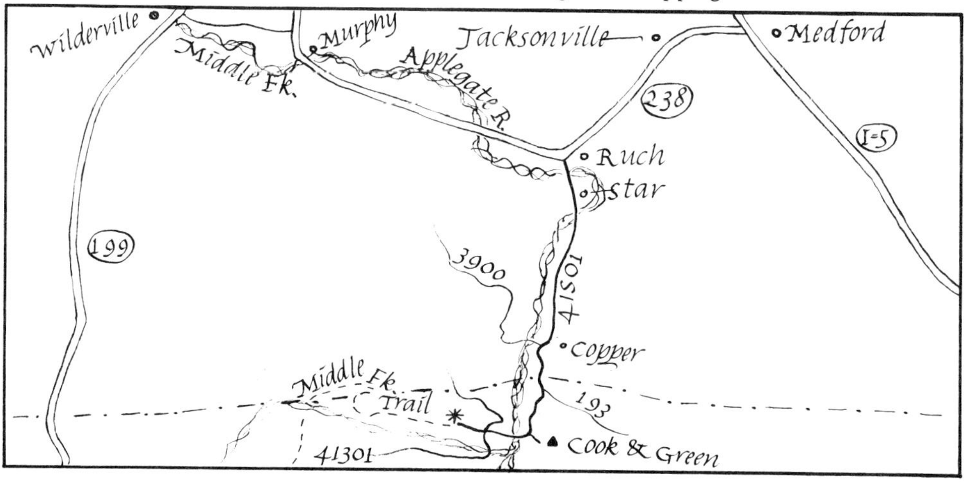

24 EIGHT DOLLAR MOUNTAIN ROAD TO ONION CAMP

Siskiyou National Forest

Drive: 36 miles from Grants Pass

Road: Partly paved; mostly gravel in fair condition

Hikes: Chetco Pass Trail, Onion Camp Trail

Features: Picnicking, camping, lake access, wilderness area

The pleasure and excitement of this trip arise from the diversity of scenery and terrain available in this part of southern Oregon. The beautiful country ranges from the dense, fir forests south of Grants Pass, to an extraordinary view of the snow-capped Siskiyous, and finally to the pre-ice age geology and vegetation typical of parts of the Kalmiopsis Wilderness.

A great part of the beauty involved in this trip is the drive along U.S. 199, which begins in Grants Pass. Otherwise known as the Redwood Highway, U.S. 199 extends south to Crescent City, California, where it merges with U.S. 101. While you see no redwoods on your way to Onion Camp, you do see shady fir forests as well as hilly farm country; you also cross the Applegate River, and pass a little spot called, delightfully, Wonder, Oregon. As you continue south, the craggy Siskiyous are everpresent on the skyline.

About 3½ miles south of Selma, turn right on Eight Dollar Mountain Road; it is 17 miles to the Kalmiopsis Wilderness. The road becomes gravel in a mile or so as it enters the national forest. Follow the Illinois River for about 3 miles on USFS 3807 before turning onto USFS 3843. As you gain elevation, look down at the startlingly green Illinois as it makes its way through a small but lush valley dotted with farms. The mountains will be in sight most of the drive, until the road descends in the direction of Onion Camp, which is one mile from the wilderness boundary. The last quarter mile of road is somewhat rough so use caution.

Creek on Onion Camp Trail

Onion Camp is named for a very obvious reason; it is the site of two half-acre or more patches of wild onions. These plants are bright green in spring, and doubtless present a memorable sight and fragrance later in the season, when in bloom. The boggy onion patches partially surround the three camp sites of Onion Camp.

Chetco Pass Trail

Follow the trail marker near the center of Onion Camp which indicates the distance to Fall Creek Trail (one-half mile) and to Chetco Pass (4½ miles). We suggest taking the trail for at least a mile, which enables you to see the unique geology and botany of the Kalmiopsis Wilderness Area while skirting the wilderness area boundary. (See Trip 15 for further explanation of the Kalmiopsis Wilderness Area.)

Walk uphill from the campground and follow Fall Creek for a short distance. The trail switchbacks several times in the first half mile but is not steep. It levels out for a distance before emerging from the trees, where you can see the surrounding mountains covered with green forests, and hear the distant sound of the Illinois River.

Contour up the side of an increasingly rocky hill, and as you near the top, enter a landscape in total contrast to the surrounding mountains. Here, the ground is covered with bolders, reddish gravel and glossy serpentine. The vegetation is sparse and grows out of cracks in the rock. The few pines have been so disfigured by the soil, weather and age that they are twisted into grotesque shapes. It is an eerie setting but strangely peaceful.

We suggest stopping here at the top, with Whetstone Butte (4,464 feet) to the right. The trail continues along the ridge for several more miles to Chetco Pass. If you plan to go much farther, carry water, for little is available along the way.

There is no single reason why the Kalmiopsis area has produced such an unusual terrain. In part, the high elevation and weather have been responsible, as well as the geological age of the area. Located in the Siskiyou Range, the rock formations of the Kalmiopsis are much older (Mesozoic or older) than those found either in the adjoining Coast or Cascade ranges. Along with great geological age has come what the Forest Service calls "a caprice of nature," mysteriously allowing several pre-ice age species of trees and shrubs to survive into the present day. Among these, the exceedingly rare *Kalmiopsis leachiana* and weeping spruce are the most famous, and are given special protection by the Forest Service. No plant or part of a plant may be taken without written permission from the Forest Service.

Onion Camp Trail

While this trail also begins at Onion Camp, it provides a distinct contrast in scenery and terrain to that found along the Chetco Pass Trail. The Onion Camp Trail winds through dramatic forest and mountain terrain before it drops down to Babyfoot Lake and the surrounding botanical study area. The distance to Babyfoot Lake is over 3 miles. Since little of the hike is on level ground, and the final one-half mile is difficult in places, the trail should not be attempted in its entirety by novice hikers. Babyfoot Lake is located within the Kalmiopsis Wilderness Area, so you should check with the Illinois Valley Ranger Station in Cave Junction about wilderness area permits.

Follow Trail 1205 south out of Onion Camp. The first 2½ miles of the trail are along an old mining road. For approximately a mile the trail continues downhill, crossing several creeks and deeply eroded gullies. The forest begins to change from predominantly fir to a mixture of fir, madrone, hemlock and Port Orford cedar. Cross another creek and begin your ascent to a clearing on the ridgetop. From here the view takes in ridge upon ridge of mountains. Continue climbing until you see a locked gate. Pass the gate and ascend until you see a small sign on the left: "Babyfoot ½ mile." From here the trail is narrow and requires some scrambling before finally dropping to the lake.

Along the trail

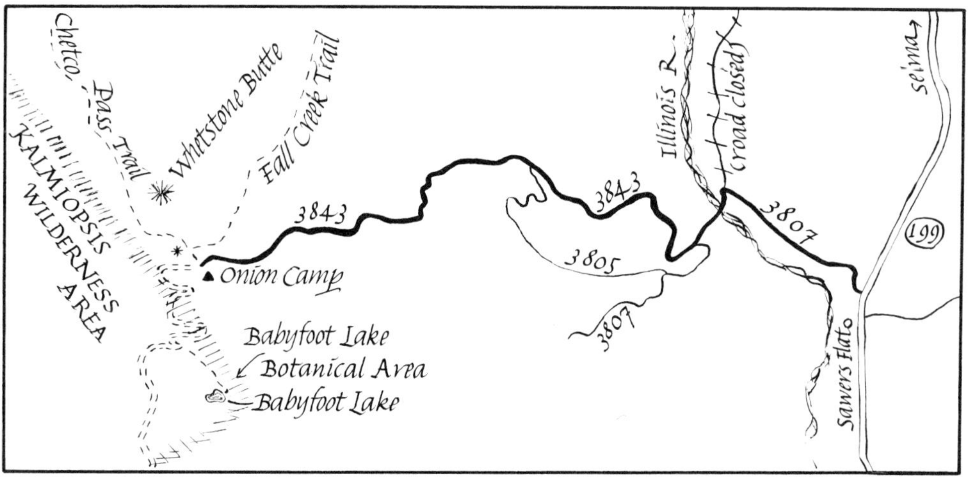

25 ILLINOIS RIVER

Siskiyou National Forest

Drive: 40 miles from Grants Pass

Road: Mostly paved; some gravel, in fair condition

Hikes: Store Gulch to Illinois River, Illinois River Trail

Features: Picnicking, camping, river and creek access

The Illinois River is sometimes deep, sometimes fast. Deep pockets of green water and fast, white slides of rapids fill the rocky canyon with the scenery and sounds of a mountain stream. While this trip begins miles away in Grants Pass, a good part of it is spent along the Illinois River.

Take U.S. 199 from Grants Pass, heading southwest about 21 miles to Selma. This part of the drive is through a flat valley, and from it you can see forested hills and some farms. The highway bypasses Wilderville but goes through the small settlement of Wonder, Oregon. Beyond Wonder, an historical marker stands at the site of Ft. Hay, and describes a Takelma Indian attack which occurred there in 1856. Farther down U.S. 199 you will pass a lumbermill, and then entering the town of Selma, you will come to the Illinois River Road, on the right, between a general store and a gas station.

Turn right onto the Illinois River Road (USFS 3504). A sign at the junction indicates that it is 10 miles to Store Gulch. While the pavement soon ends, the gravel road is fairly good, and the intriguing interplay of fir forest, river, canyon, rock and sky may make the drive seem much shorter than it is. Before Store Gulch there are two or three picknicking/campsites at Little Six Mile Creek. At Store Gulch, on the right, is a guard station with bark siding. Across the road is the Store Gulch Campground, where there is water, a pit toilet, camping, picnicking and a trail to the river.

Store Gulch to Illinois River

This short, well maintained trail switchbacks down the canyon wall to the river. The trail is gentle, safe and easier than it looks from the top, although the very end can be tricky as the trail disappears and you have to scramble five or ten yards to the canyon floor. Keep small children back from the edge, and use caution at the trail end. This trail takes you to a good swimming and fishing hole, and a small gravel sunbathing beach.

The next trail is somewhat more of a walk. Nine miles beyond Store Gulch, USFS 3504 deadends at the Illinois River Trail and Campground. Continuing along the river, the road passes two sideroads for river access parking. Then this stretch of road climbs above the green Illinois River, and drops to river level for more access to the water. Finally the road forks. To the left is a private drive, and to the right is the trailhead. This last piece of road may be too rough for a sedan. Unless the road appears well maintained, park at the bottom and walk to the trailhead. A campground with pit toilets is at the end of the road, as is the beginning of the Illinois River Trail.

Illinois River Trail

Cross the footbridge at the end of the campground, and then follow the trail as it gently climbs through the forest, curves, and then drops to Panther Creek. Take the footbridge across this small, swift mountain stream and then you will soon climb again as the trail skirts the Illinois River canyon. Good views of the river are frequent along this stretch of trail, but although you can see and hear the river far below, there is no access to it. Within 2 miles from the Panther Creek Bridge, the trail leads through the York Creek Area, a designated and protected botanical study area. Whether you walk to the bridge, or beyond, the Illinois River Trail will lead you through a beautiful part of the country.

Illinois River

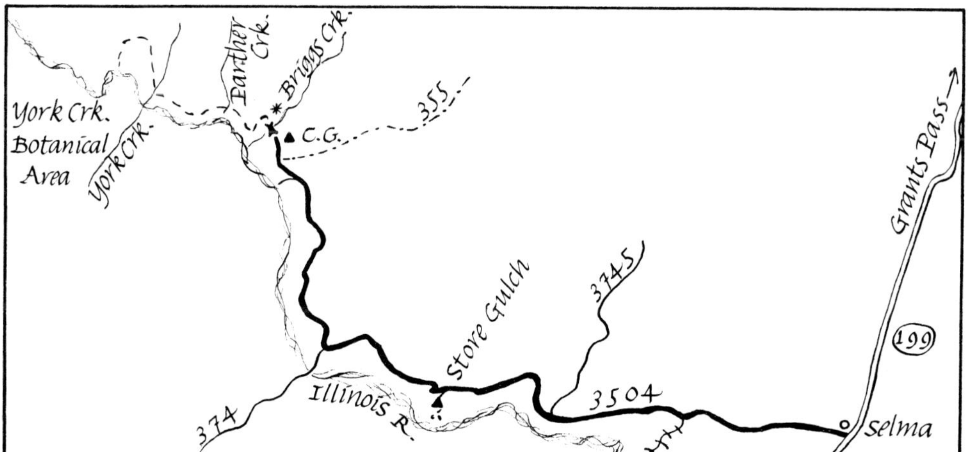

Cover photo by Ira Spring
Sawtooth Ridge from Salmon River Valley

Maps: Susan Hawkins

Map Lettering: Dennis Bleything

Editor: Thomas K. Worcester